To, Chris

With best wishes.

Richard

HEDGE FUNDS

An introduction to

SKILL BASED

INVESTMENT STRATEGIES

RICHARD HILLS

HEDGE
FUNDS

An introduction to

SKILL BASED

INVESTMENT STRATEGIES

RICHARD HILLS

RUSHMERE WYNNE

First published 1996

British Library Cataloguing in Publication Data.
A catalogue record for this book is available from the British Library.

ISBN 0 948035 28 5

Designed by MacWing

Published by:
Rushmere Wynne Limited
4-5 Harmill, Grovebury Road,
Leighton Buzzard
Bedfordshire LU7 8FF
Tel: 01525 853726
Fax: 01525 852037

Printed by:
BOOKCRAFT Book Printers & Binders
First Avenue, Westfield Trading Estate,
Midsomer Norton, Bath, Avon BA3 4BS

ACKNOWLEDGEMENTS

In the writing of this book I realise that I have placed a great many demands on people around me in achieving what I hope is a worthwhile result. It has also been necessary to ensure the technical accuracy and in this area I am particularly grateful to a number of old friends and former colleagues in the City of London and further afield who have so willingly and diligently given their time to this project. Their comments have on many occasions been staggeringly incisive and perceptive. I would like to thank in particular the following for their contribution:

Simon Aldis, freelance writer, who has read the book through the eyes of a layman.

Dan Bunting, Investment Strategist, Matheson Securities Limited, for his unparalleled knowledge of all investment matters coupled with a very keen editorial eye.

Victor Hill, Managing Director, International Management Development, who provided a ruthlessly rigorous testing of many of the looser comments in early drafts.

Peter Hiscocks, Managing Director, Integral Europe Limited and his team for producing some of the statistical figures quoted.

Anthea Nugent, Head of Manager Research, William M. Mercer Limited, who, despite being well down the approach path to the birth of her son Henry, still found time to read the manuscript and make many improvements and offer encouraging remarks all round.

Peter Warrington, Director of Sales and Marketing, The WM Company, for his very friendly advice and help in providing statistics on the UK pensions market.

Barrett Wissman, Managing Director, Hunt & Wissman, who provided valuable insight into the trading strategies of Infinity Investors Limited and who is a store of information on the practical side of hedge fund investing.

Leslie A. Balzer, Investment Manager, Lend Lease Investment Management of Sydney, Australia, for expanding my knowledge of the Post Modern Portfolio Theory. Some of my text in Chapter 4 is based on his award-winning article in *The Journal of Investing* published in 1994.

Brian M. Rom and Kathleen W. Ferguson, respectively President and Principal of Sponsor-Software Systems Inc., New York, for their permission to reproduce several charts used to explain the Post Modern Portfolio Theory.

Finally, an extra big "thank you" is due to **George Van,** Chairman of Van Hedge Advisors, Inc. of Nashville, Tennessee, who so generously and freely provided access to his hedge fund indices and other statistics on the size and growth of the hedge fund industry which have helped so much to add depth to this book and state the case for hedge funds.

I am also aware that I have placed extra strain and responsibility on my staff at Argyll Investment Management Limited and would like to take this opportunity of thanking **Emma Beebe** in particular for her hard work in collecting and checking data and various proofs of this book.

The City of London has always been a great centre of innovation and free thinking and although today hedge funds lay buried under a coating of mistrust and misunderstanding I am sure their value will be recognised in the years ahead. The support and encouragement of my City friends underlines the willingness of people to listen to the debate.

I have tried hard to ensure that the presentation of hedge funds in this book is as clear as possible. However we are dealing with a relatively new concept and if you, the reader, at any time feel unclear as to the explanations given, please feel free to write to me at Argyll Investment Management Limited, 60 Queen Anne Street, London, W1M 9LA with your queries. I should however make it clear that I cannot provide specific investment advice and in this respect you should consult your own investment adviser.

Richard Hills
London
April 1996

WEALTH WARNING

Whilst all reasonable care has been taken to ensure that the details in this book are true and not misleading at the time of publication, no liability is accepted by Rushmere Wynne nor Richard Hills nor their servants or agents, for the use of information contained herein in any circumstances connected with actual trading or otherwise. Neither Rushmere Wynne nor Richard Hills nor their servants or agents are responsible for any errors or omissions within this book. It is published for information purposes only and shall not constitute investment advice. All descriptions, examples and calculations contained in this book are for guidance purposes only and should not be treated as definitive.

Certain investments or investment services mentioned in this book may not be suitable for all readers and further advice should be sought from your Investment Adviser in this respect. Please note that the value of investments and the income derived from them may fall as well as rise and you may get back less than originally invested. Past performance is not necessarily a guide to future performance.

* * *

CONTENTS

DEFINITION OF A HEDGE FUND

*There is a Glossary of important terms and definitions on pages 201–205. The terms in **bold** are explained in the Glossary.*

Everyone knows the term "hedging your bets". It means that you make a number of bets to cover all eventualities so that you end up winning, no matter what. That is really what **hedge funds** are about; devising strategies to minimise investment risk, and deliver a profit, whatever happens. The term "**hedge fund**" is used to cover a broad range of funds adopting different strategies in different markets.

Some characteristics are common to all hedge funds –

1. The primary aim of a hedge fund is to produce **absolute returns,** adjusted to bear the lowest risk possible for that target return. This applies whether the fund is seeking high, medium, or low returns. Traditional investment funds are different. They generally measure progress in relative terms, comparing it with some benchmark, often a market index like the FT-SE 100. Traditional funds are less concerned with the level of risk they take on, and content merely to beat their benchmark. This may often mean that, perhaps unwittingly, they take higher risks than their target return would warrant.

2. Since hedge funds are aiming for the best **risk-adjusted returns,** they must seek to control the level of potential gain or loss. Over time, this is achieved by varying their net exposure to the markets. This is done by controlling **long** and **short positions** and using **futures, options** and other strategies to minimise the volatility of their portfolio. It may mean surrendering some potential gains in exchange for limiting any possible losses.

3. Hedge fund managers are paid in a different way to conventional fund managers. Investing for absolute returns is much more demanding than simply seeking relative returns. Running a hedge fund requires a much greater range of skill and knowledge, and tends to attract only the more enterprising and

talented managers. They are rewarded by high fees which are linked to performance. A manager who performs well and beats a specific **absolute benchmark** can earn up to 25% of that gain, but receives no performance fee if there is no **absolute return**. The conventional **long-only manager** will charge a fixed annual fee whether he performs well or not.

4. Hedge funds generally have a different structure to traditional unit trusts or investment trusts. Because they use more sophisticated financial techniques and instruments, they tend to be based in tax free areas where financial regulation allows greater freedom. The biggest exception is the large number of domestic US hedge funds which are set up as **limited partnerships.** These escape regulation by the US Securities and Exchange Commission when there are fewer than 100 partners in the fund.

    Until the major financial centres allow funds to use **gearing** and **short-selling** freely in pooled vehicles, the hedge fund industry will be concentrated in off-shore centres.

In conclusion, hedge funds are investment vehicles which seek **absolute returns.** They are managed by entrepreneurial managers, and are based in tax free, less regulated areas. They seek the highest returns compatible with a measured degree of risk, employing techniques which are not usually used in conventional, **long-only** investing. These may involve **short-selling, arbitrage, options, futures** and **gearing** in a carefully constructed investment strategy.

A Simple Hedge Fund Strategy

Investor H decides that the stockmarket will be generally flat over the next quarter, but while the market is likely to trade sideways there are certain shares with the potential to rise sharply.

In order to benefit from his ability as a **stock-picker** Investor H creates a classic hedge fund by buying the shares he thinks will rise, and hedging against a fall in the market by selling FT-SE 100 Index Futures.

In order to maximise his gains, he would like to buy more shares than he can afford, so he borrows extra funds from the bank. Starting with £10,000, he borrows a further £20,000. He then buys £30,000 of shares, and simultaneously sells £25,000 of Index Futures. He must sell sufficient of the Index Futures virtually to match the amount of his equity investments. Otherwise he has capital of just £10,000, but £30,000 at risk in shares. By selling £25,000 of Index Futures, he only has £5,000 – 50% of his own capital – exposed to market risk (see the equation below). Yet his exposure to potential share price gains is £30,000 – three times his starting capital.

$$\text{Market exposure} = \frac{(\text{Long share exposure} - \text{Short index exposure})}{\text{Capital}} \times 100$$

$$= \frac{(30{,}000 - 25{,}000)}{10{,}000} \times 100 = 50\%$$

Some weeks later the shares he bought have risen by 5% while the stockmarket has remained static. The investor makes the following return:

$$£30{,}000 \times 5\% = £1{,}500$$

Interest charges on the £20,000 of borrowings are offset partly by the **cost of carry premium** which the investor receives when he sells Index Futures. If, for simplicity, we ignore all these actual and implied costs and benefits, Investor H has made a return of £1,500 on capital of £10,000 or 15%. By using gearing coupled with Index Futures to keep total market exposure, and therefore risk, to £5,000, the investor has been able to take an equity position three times bigger than his capital base.

In contrast, a traditional **long-only manager** with capital of £10,000 buying the same shares would have only made £500 and yet his net exposure to the stockmarket, and hence risk, would have been £10,000 at all times or twice that of the hedge fund manager.

If the stockmarket had fallen during the period by 10% Investor H would have been protected by his short Index Futures position. He sold this for £25,000 but was able to buy it back 10% cheaper for £22,500. Assuming the shares he held fell by only 5% the overall outcome would still have been positive by £1,000.

$$\begin{aligned} \text{Net gain} &= \text{Loss on shares} + \text{Gain on short Index Futures exposure} \\ &= (30{,}000 \times 0.95) - 30{,}000 + 25{,}000 - (25{,}000 \times 0.9) = £1{,}000 \end{aligned}$$

* * *

INTRODUCTION

Hedge funds are the investment industry's last great secret, a source of stunning performance and yet largely unknown and unappreciated by most investors.

Hedge funds started 50 years ago. Now there are nearly 5,000 of them, looking after more than US$300 billion on behalf of wealthy and well-informed clients. Over the longer term they have generated results which far outshine those from more conventional investments. Between 1988 and 1995, hedge funds achieved a net compound annual return of 18.4%, nearly double the 9.9% return from the FT/S&P Actuaries World Index. Some of the higher risk funds have generated gains which are little short of extraordinary. Yet private investors in the UK hardly know of their existence, and many professional fund managers barely understand them.

This is about to change. Hedge funds are poised to move into the mainstream. In the next five years they will begin to command a place in many professional portfolios. A decade from now many people will appreciate the sense of holding some proportion of their assets in hedge funds. **The rewards will be high for those who understand the potential.** As always, the greatest returns are likely to go to those who take the trouble to learn what is happening, and who make the first move.

An Open Mind

This book will help those who are prepared to approach the subject with an open mind, seeking to gain a proper understanding of the potential and the pitfalls of hedge funds. In the UK today the mention of hedge funds is apt to bring an immediate and negative reaction from most investment professionals. All too often, they say, "We don't touch them. We're investors, not speculators." That reflects the conventional notion that such funds are high-risk, gambling vehicles. It is an attitude born of ignorance. What people do not understand, they often mistrust.

Where hedge funds have found their way into popular consciousness, the media have labelled them speculative, reporting only a few of the most spectacular coups or setbacks, ignoring the vast volume of good solid achievement attained by most in the business. Since there are few reliable sources of information readily available, most people have no reason to challenge this misconception. As with many things in life, perception and reality are distant cousins.

The reality is that the classic hedge fund is primarily concerned with reducing market risk by limiting the downside and allowing the investment skill of the managers to shine through so capturing gains even when a falling market is taking conventional funds lower.

This book sets out to dispel the myths and explain the reality. We look first at the history of hedge funds, and how the industry has developed in recent years. Next we investigate some of the strategies the funds pursue, then we take a close look at some of the best-known names in the business and a few of the exciting new ones who are just emerging.

The second half of the book sets the scene for an objective discussion of risk and return by looking at how our understanding of this apparently straightforward concept has been developed and refined in recent years. **Modern Portfolio Theory** laid the foundations for risk/return analysis. Now, with the advent of **Post Modern Portfolio Theory,** we have an even more powerful tool to compare more objectively than ever the risk/return characteristics of different assets. We can demonstrate mathematically the relative benefits of investing in a fund whether conventional or hedged. In addition managers now have a much more accurate weapon to allow them to measure their investment risk and to take action to control it.

We move on to examine the similarities and differences between conventional funds and hedge funds; how to access these funds and how to assess them. This allows us to go on to look at the best ways to construct a portfolio of hedge funds taking into account the strengths and weaknesses of individual management styles. Then we examine whether hedge funds are suitable for all investors and close with a brief view of how the future of hedge funds might develop.

A Profit Whatever Happens

Hedging is about laying off risk. When you hedge your bets, you exploit movements in the odds, making a variety of bets which will cover all eventualities, and hopefully leave you with a profit, whatever the result. **That, in essence, is what the classic hedge fund strives for – devising strategies to minimise investment risk so capturing the gains in any investment situation and ensuring a profit whatever happens.**

If that sounds too good to be true, the ideal, unattainable investment, so be it.

The classic hedge fund which can guarantee gains in any circumstances does not yet exist. Or, if it does, we have yet to find it. But there are many hedge funds which seek to operate with something similar in mind. The elimination or drastic reduction of risk is central to the hedge fund proper, and is the most crucial factor which distinguishes hedge funds from conventional funds.

Hedge funds seek to reduce or eliminate market risk by attempting to maximise the impact of the investment skills of the manager. A conventional long-only fund will only hold investments – securities of some sort – and will not normally shake off the influence of the general market trend. It is generally considered that the underlying behaviour of the market accounts for 80% of a conventional, active fund's return. This leaves a mere 20% of performance attributable to the inherent skills of the manager. That is just as well perhaps, since only about a quarter of unit trusts beat their benchmark index – a disconcerting commentary on the skills of the managers.

Hedge funds are different. They are not judged by achieving better returns than the herd by gaining more or losing less. **Hedge funds seek to capture absolute gains at all times** whether in a rising, static or falling market. Not for them the dismal pretence of doing well by limiting the fund to a fall of 15% in a market which may have dropped 20%. For the client, a loss is a loss, whether it is less than the average or not. Hedge funds set themselves a more demanding task. For them, a loss is a loss, whatever the reason.

Within that framework, hedge funds vary considerably in the risks they take, and the rewards they offer. Many attempt to hedge out market risk completely, and rely for performance wholly on the ability of the manager to buy and sell investments profitably. They do this by using a variety of devices. In its simplest form, a hedge fund is distinguished from a typical unit trust or investment trust by its ability to sell short – sell investments it does not own in the hope of being able to buy them back more cheaply at a future date. (Short-selling is explained fully in *Profit of the Plunge* by Simon Cawkwell, published by Rushmere Wynne, 1995, paperback, £9.99 ISBN 0-948035-17-X.)

Short-Selling – A Difficult Concept

Many investors might find this a difficult concept to understand, let alone practise. It is much easier to see how you can be long of an investment, how you can actually own it, than to sell something you do not own. And it appears less risky. If you own an investment that becomes worthless, all you have lost is your capital. If you sell an investment short, you must buy it back at some point to close the deal. The price could rise against you, and keep rising, threatening an infinite loss. Catastrophic, but improbable in the real world. Or there could be a takeover bid to send the price soaring against you.

The sensible hedge fund manager, however, is well aware of the dangers. Because he or she is much more acutely concerned than the conventional manager with measuring risk, stop losses will have been put in place, with a prudent limit on the size of each individual short position, keeping potential losses within acceptable levels. Such safeguards are the essence of a classic hedge fund.

Selling short and using stop loss positions are among the simplest devices employed by hedge fund managers. In modern financial markets, there is an almost infinite variety of devices open to the sophisticated manager, with futures and derivatives merely part of the armoury. As the search for exceptional returns has spread over a wider range, and as some of the most successful funds have grown to a size which means they must commit to very large deals if they are to generate high returns, the nature of hedge funds has become more varied and their methods have strayed from the original classic basis of hedge fund operations. A few have moved away from the notion of purely minimising risk, and have begun to seek out more speculative situations, coming closer to higher-risk gambling funds. Inevitably, these attract more attention for their successes or failures, and have muddied the image of the whole hedge fund movement. Though they may be called hedge funds in popular parlance, they barely qualify under the original term, and do a disservice to the perception of the vast mass of funds which operate in a more traditional mould.

A Wide Range Of Styles

There are nearly 5,000 hedge funds worldwide. They cover a broad spectrum of risk levels, and employ a wide variety of investment instruments, long and short. At one extreme, there are futures funds which trade exclusively in stock index and commodity futures. These are often, but not always, highly geared, speculative vehicles. They set out to produce exceptional returns, and can cope with high levels of volatility resulting from such strategies. They are not, strictly speaking, hedge funds, because they do not hedge out market risk.

Next come the macro players, people like George Soros, who look to gain from major financial events, using either long or short positions. Such funds seek to profit by exploiting events which occur when political decisions generate unsustainable tensions in financial markets. As the tensions are released, there is the opportunity for gain. The classic example is the way in which Soros sold short of Sterling late in 1992, effectively helping to force the UK out of the European Exchange Rate Mechanism.

Along with the futures funds, the macro players have captured the imagination of the press, and their exploits or misadventures are apt to hit the headlines. The stories foster the notion that anyone buying into such hedge funds is doing little more than taking a spin on the roulette wheel. That is not true; the strategies such players pursue are constructed carefully, with a far higher likelihood of success than the random chance of a spin of the wheel.

Unfortunately, the ballyhoo creates a misleading impression of the world of hedge funds. Only 4% of all hedge funds are macro funds, taking big positions to exploit the outcome of major events. The majority of hedge fund managers work in medium to low-risk areas. They are highly disciplined investors seeking returns from a variety of carefully considered strategies. Many are involved in arbitrage trading, a strategy with limited downside where perhaps an undervalued convertible loan stock might be bought, while selling a corresponding amount of ordinary shares. This sort of conservative policy is employed by many low-risk managers who seek to pick up small incremental gains from arbitrage trades, generating returns marginally above those on short-dated bonds.

Though their approach might appear unfamiliar, such funds actually carry less risk than most unit trusts when set against the conventional investment yardstick of standard deviation – the statistical measure of the spread of risk which is used to estimate the variability of future returns. Once again, this focuses on the key role of a hedge fund manager in assessing exactly how much risk he is taking with the assets in his fund, and then in seeking to keep that risk within defined limits. High-risk hedge fund managers may justifiably be classed as speculators. It is wrong, however, to assume that all hedge fund managers are high-risk players.

This is in marked and, perhaps, surprising contrast to the approach of the conventional unit trust manager. He is rarely concerned with risk management, and does not generally quantify the risks he is taking. His role is to outperform a benchmark, some form of index, or industry median. In practice, many unit trust managers are content to stay in the middle, following the herd. This may be difficult enough, but is less taxing than the task facing a hedge fund manager. And that may explain why there is such a difference in the financial rewards for the two sets of managers.

Huge Rewards For Success

The conventional pooled investment fund charges a fee of around 1.5% a year. The average hedge fund manager adds to this a performance related fee of perhaps 25% on all new gains. So the rewards for success are potentially huge, particularly since many management companies are owned by just one individual. In the UK, for instance, Crispin Odey moved from Barings, where he was highly acclaimed as a conventional fund manager. He set up his own hedge fund, and in his first year, his earnings soared from over £100,000 to some £19 million. After one good year, he hit a disastrous patch. There may be room for debate over whether such fees are justified, but clients do pay them.

Though Odey and a few others have had their problems, the high fee structure endorses the attractions of hedge funds. Sophisticated investors with access to the best advice are willing to pay massive performance fees. They would not do so unless the funds delivered value. Such investors do not continue paying for second rate performance. And the size of the prize ensures a constant flow of the best management talent into hedge funds.

The industry is dominated by individuals with truly exceptional intelligence and experience. Money talks. It attracts the top talent. The level of investment sophistication among hedge fund operators is way above that of the average money manager. Top hedge operators inhabit a different world, using a range of techniques and disciplines not available to conventional managers, who must appear blinkered by comparison.

Despite this, prudent investors are always well advised to spread their assets in order to reduce risk. This maxim holds good for hedge funds. Anyone seeking to produce an efficient portfolio which maximises returns while minimising risk should take in a number of hedge funds. The criteria for selecting the ideal mix are complex and varied, and we discuss them in this book.

A Balanced Selection Of Funds

In essence, we are concerned with achieving a balanced selection of funds, with the risk profile of each being set off against the others. The lower the correlation of risk between individual funds, the lower the overall volatility of the combined portfolio. To produce the optimal portfolio it is necessary to consider how each fund achieves its returns, and to seek a portfolio with a well-spread range of investment styles. It is possible to achieve excellent results by applying careful and systematic analysis.

In 1994, hedge funds suffered from the collapse of the bond market, and many lost money for their clients. There was talk of irreparable damage to the industry shattering the confidence of investors. In July 1995, George Soros wrote to his clients, telling them of a change in emphasis, and a refocusing across his funds. Bruce Kovner and Paul Tudor Jones, two more legendary managers, decided to reduce the size of their funds, and to return some money to clients. Michael Steinhardt, another of the industry giants, went one step further. He decided he had had enough, and announced in October 1995 that he was closing down completely. He returned money to clients early in 1996.

Though these moves generated a rash of sceptical comments, the worst predictions have proved ill-founded. Leading funds bounced back strongly in 1995 as we show below:

LEADING HEDGE FUND MANAGER'S PERFORMANCE 1994/95		
	1994	1995
	%	%
George Soros – Quantum Fund	3	49
Michael Steinhardt	– 28	23
Julian Robertson	–7	14

A number of new funds have been started over the past 12 months. Following a good 1995 we expect the industry to grow further in 1996 and beyond.

Hedge funds have their place in modern investment, independently, or as part of a conventional portfolio. The benefits they can bring to a conventional portfolio by reducing risk and enhancing returns should make them an automatic choice. Given the rising tide of worry about the levels of the London and Wall Street markets as we go through 1996 and beyond, the attractions of funds which seek to control market risk and achieve positive returns against any background must be considerably enhanced.

This book concentrates on the hedge fund industry today. As a result there is a heavy slant towards the US where the industry is widely developed and accepted. There are hedge fund managers in the UK but due to the constraints of the Financial Services Act 1986 coupled with taxation and advertising issues the funds themselves are based offshore. This may change as legislation moves forward and as UK pension schemes start to use hedge funds.

In the years ahead, as more investors come to concentrate on the importance of measuring risk, and of matching returns to a given level of risk, pressure will be exerted on traditional fund managers to produce better risk-adjusted results. Conventional wisdom could be reversed. As the understanding of risk increases, traditional long-only managers and their limited range of investment techniques may come under the spotlight. There may be questions about just who is taking the unquantified risks and who are the real speculators.

Until there is a greater understanding of how the hedge fund industry really works, misapprehensions will persist. Hopefully, this book will help dispel some of the mystique by presenting hedge funds in a more objective fashion showing that their managers are the skill-based, alternative strategists of the investment world.

1

THE HISTORY OF HEDGE FUNDS – NAILING A FEW NONSENSES

The concept of hedging is far from new. It dates back to at least the 17th century where it was being practised in both the Far East and Europe. Hedging and hedge funds are not, therefore, the new investment tools of the 1980s and 90s.

Hedging can be described as any action taken to give protection against a sudden and/or large adverse price change in a commodity in which we have an interest. This price change could be upwards or downwards, representing either an opportunity or a risk, depending on our initial position. For example, take the farmer who is growing a crop of rice. He calculates that he will make a profit if the price is above a certain level (P units) at harvest time. If the current price of rice is P+5 units per bushel, he knows that if there is no price change between now and the harvest he will make a profit of 5 units per bushel sold. He can wait until harvest to see if the price changes, but takes a risk that if it falls below P, he will make a loss on his crop. If he bought his farm with a loan which he would then be unable to service, he would lose everything. That is the risk. However, if the price of rice rises substantially to P+15, he would make a considerable profit. That is the opportunity.

What can he do to steer an even course between disaster and success? Quite clearly he must hedge a part of his risk by trading in some of his potential opportunity. As far back as the 1600s, rice farmers in Japan did just that. They would obtain from the local rice warehouse a credit note for a set quantity of rice. In return, they would be under an obligation to provide the warehouse with that same quantity of rice at harvest. The farmers would then sell the rice to a rice trader for a set price and pass over the credit note in return for payment. The trader would be free to either remove rice from the warehouse, sell the credit note, or take the rice at some time in the future. In this way, the farmers had guaranteed their selling price, and the merchant his buying price, and the warehouse would charge a fee as facilitator. All parties were happy, and the wheels of commerce were nicely oiled.

At the same time as these transactions were occurring, "Tulip Mania" was gripping Holland. The first tulips arrived in Northern Europe from Turkey in the middle of the 16th century. They became the fashion of the day. A tulip collection became one of the most visible displays of status and wealth. Different varieties began to command premium prices, and a grading system developed. By the 1620s, tulip growing had become a major industry in Holland. One inventor studied Egyptian science, and devised a mummifying machine to protect the plant. Another tale has a hapless sailor mistaking one bulb for an onion, adding it to his breakfast herring, and consuming a meal worth the equivalent of the wages of his whole ship's crew for a year.

Collectors began to hold tulip bulbs as investments and banks to take them as security. Gradually the tulip bulb became the centre of a raft of get-rich-quick schemes. As the price of bulbs soared, every self-respecting Dutch businessman had his tulip broker. A jobbing market developed with gamblers buying on every fall in price and selling on rises. Almost every household became sucked into trading and growing tulips. By the mid 1630s, special tulip markets were common. A futures market developed, with traders issuing promises to deliver bulbs later in the year. The contracts themselves were traded, and soon followed by option markets allowing speculators the right to buy or sell quantities of special bulbs at set dates. Dutch economists began to predict that the ever-increasing price of tulip bulbs would ensure prosperity for the nation's economy for years to come.

Finally, the bubble burst. Tulips were no longer being grown in gardens, but were bought to sell on again. As sceptical voices grew louder, the boom reversed. Universal panic took hold, and dealers began to default. Charles Mackay in the 19th century classic *Extraordinary Popular Delusions and the Madness of Crowds*[1] gives an example of how a dealer had agreed a futures contract to buy a particular bulb at four thousand florins, only to find the price had slumped to three or four hundred florins when the six-week contract expired. He refused to honour it as a cry of distress sounded across the nation. In the end, it was agreed in Amsterdam that all contracts made at the height of the mania, or before November 1636, should be declared null and void, upsetting all those left holding stocks of bulbs. The matter

1. Available from *the Investors' book club*, tel: 0171 247 4557

was finally referred to the Provincial Council at The Hague, but no court could find a solution. Prices slumped, even though minor tulip mania then spread to London and Paris. Even today, tulip prices are not back to 1636 levels. The speculative bubble left bankrupts all over Holland, plunged the nation into a depression, and damaged its financial credibility around the world for decades.

From such early beginnings, the use of hedging developed in the farming and commodities markets. By the early part of this century, it was possible to trade most major hard and soft commodities on spot and futures markets. The producers would sell their production forward to lock in a known price and profit, safeguarding themselves against a fall in prices. The consumer industry or wholesalers would buy forward to protect themselves against price rises and consequent losses. As time went on, a new breed of player entered the market, the professional speculator. He saw the opportunity to make money by acting as a facilitator and risk-taker. In his first role, he provided liquidity by being prepared to take the other side of transactions in the market where without him there would be no buyer or seller to match the position. His reward was to strike a deal at a more advantageous rate than otherwise possible. His second role, as a speculator, was to take positions, long or short, in the market where he could see an opportunity to make a profit as prices moved his way.

Market activity was further increased in this century by the gradual move to standardise futures contracts in terms of the amount of produce traded. As more markets opened up in the US, the UK, the Continent of Europe and the Far East, so the ability to arbitrage between one market and another became available. For instance, suppose the price of 6 month forward wheat in Chicago is US$X per tonne and in London £Y per tonne. After allowing for the exchange rate calculation and differential delivery costs, it may be that the price of wheat in London is lower than in Chicago, so a trader could buy in London, sell in Chicago, and make an instant paper profit. Hopefully over the next 6 months, before delivery is due, prices in both centres would come back into line, and the positions could be closed out by buying back the short position in Chicago and then selling the long London position. In such a way, a profit would be crystallised without the need to take delivery of the commodity, the wheat. This pure paper transaction is a good example of a space arbitrage, the buying and selling in two different locations of the same commodity to benefit from price differences.

Trading in wheat was notable for one particular deal in the thirties. One afternoon in 1931, a partner at a London broking firm (since a casualty of the October 1986 London Stock Exchange *Big Bang*) was called up by a client, John Maynard Keynes. He wanted to buy wheat, but specifically on a US exchange. It was late in the afternoon, and the partner was in a rush to go home, so he quickly wired the order out to the States. Just as he was leaving the office, he thought that he ought, for good form, to hedge out the currency risk by buying US$ to match the contract value and selling the corresponding amount of £s. Overnight sterling came off the gold standard. It fell against the US$, resulting in a large £ profit on the wheat position. How prescient of the partner to hedge the currency at a time when stability was the watchword and exchange rates hardly moved from day to day. How clever it was of Keynes, who had been an adviser to HM Treasury, to speculate and go long of US$

denominated wheat. It would be interesting to see what would happen if this transaction were to occur in today's heavily regulated environment.

Only in the past 20 years have we seen the advent of financial futures and a proliferation of contracts, ranging from short sterling to the FT-SE 100. There are now 22 futures and options contracts traded daily on the London International Financial Futures Exchange (LIFFE) related solely to financial products, plus a further 71 equity options on single companies. This pattern is mirrored in Chicago and the other major world exchanges. Some financial futures contracts which are based on one exchange are dealt in an almost fungible or interchangeable form on another. Effectively these contracts are identical, and can be delivered on more than one market. If you are long one contract on exchange A and short one contract on exchange B, the contracts can be netted off to zero without having to be closed out at maturity, thus opening up the opportunity of 24 hour world-wide trading. An example of this is the Eurodollar contract traded on the Chicago Mercantile Exchange and the Singapore Monetary Exchange where mutual offsetting of positions is allowed.

A whole new esoteric world of financial instruments trading has grown up. The operators often have mathematics degrees as well as post-graduate qualifications. It is not so much the fact of the instruments themselves being complex, as the way in which they are combined to create complex multifaceted synthetic derivatives of derivatives which require the skills of such highly qualified people.

The traditional long-only equity investor now has instruments available to him which allow exposure to the whole market, or elements of it, to be completely or partially hedged out by:

- Selling sufficient financial index futures to cover the value of the portfolio.

- Selling index options to cover the value of the portfolio.

- Buying puts or selling calls on the individual components of the portfolio.

The added manoeuvrability available to today's investors is huge compared to 20 years ago but it is still under-utilised by many.

The larger banks and brokers are often willing to construct specific instruments for investors with special requirements. These instruments are not tradeable across the exchanges, but are nevertheless invaluable tools to the highly specialist manager. As an example, let us suppose a fund manager wishes to go short of the European chemical sector in proportion to each company's weighting in the FT/S&P – Actuaries Europe Index. It would be very time consuming and difficult to do this. But in one transaction with a major broker, he could obtain a contract with both a fixed strike price and specific duration to cover it. The ease, relative cheapness and pure feasibility makes such tailor-made derivatives very valuable.

It is difficult in practice for private investors to sell stock short, although it is less of a problem for institutional fund managers. In the US, private and institutional investors have been shorting stocks for years. This may in part explain why hedge funds have been much quicker to catch on in the US than here. If UK investment managers wish to short the market, they have no difficulty. But if they wish to short individual stocks, they must borrow from the market the stock they have sold in order to deliver it to the buyer. UK market makers, in contrast, have always been allowed to go short of stock without having to borrow it back. Now they have created a new niche for themselves by offering fund managers synthetic short stock positions. However, they charge a hefty interest rate over the London Interbank Offer Rate (LIBOR) for the privilege. Brokers sell managers specific short contracts in many stocks, then sell these stocks in the market to balance their books. This satisfies the manager's needs and makes a nice risk-free profit for the broker.

THE HISTORY OF HEDGE FUNDS

Let us now look more specifically at hedge funds and their history. The original concept was not created by the rocket scientists and computer wizards of the 1980s and 90s. In fact, the first hedge fund, designed to control a portfolio's investment risk, was created by a remarkable American (although Australian by birth), Alfred Jones. Born in 1901, he died aged 88 in 1989.

Jones is widely accepted as the father of hedge funds and formed his first fund in 1949. Compared to the complexity of some of today's funds, his was based on a beautifully simple idea, easy to understand and with few elements. He wanted to cut out the influence of market movements on his portfolio (systematic risk) so that he would only be left with risk connected directly to the stock he held (non-systematic risk). By achieving this, he would be able to claim that all performance was due to his particular stock picking skills. And he could eliminate the problems of market timing when new funds were available for investment. What Jones achieved in his model, shown below, was a quantum leap in financial engineering:

$$\text{Market Exposure} = \frac{(\text{Long exposure} - \text{Short exposure})}{\text{Capital}}$$

The above equation in itself is not particularly earth shattering. Capital for a given portfolio is fixed and market exposure is a variable dependent on the net long/short exposure of the portfolio. Jones was undoubtedly a talented stock-picker, but he also understood the inherent risks in investing. The key to his work lay in the way he combined gearing and short selling of individual securities in the top line of the equation to control risk while increasing the scope for stock picking gains.

Jones geared his portfolios through borrowing, simultaneously selling short a number of individual securities to produce the required level of market exposure on his initial capital. If he could see a number of good buys and sells, he would borrow more and simultaneously buy more stocks and sell more shorts, keeping his market exposure constant. The effect of this is shown in Figure 1.1 below:

Net Market Exposure £	Capital £	Borrowings £	Long Exposure £	Short Exposure £	Value of stock positions £
800	1000	200	1200	400	1600
800	1000	400	1400	600	2000
800	1000	600	1600	800	2400
800	1000	800	1800	1000	2800

Figure 1.1 Jones's relationship between long and short-selling.

As you can see from the table (bottom right hand corner) a long/short stock-picker borrowing £800 can have £2,800 or 2.8 times his starting capital of £1,000 working for him while still only having 80% of his capital exposed to systematic stockmarket risk. Of the total invested, £800 would be exposed to stockmarket risk (systematic risk), while £2,000 would bear stock specific risk (non-systematic risk) only. This of course assumes the longs and shorts are reasonably correlated by industry sector. If this were not so, the real level of market exposure would rise. A skilled and risk conscious hedge fund manager's gains compared to a long-only manager should be good in a rising market; while in a falling market he should lose less.

This example highlights why hedge fund investment is so powerful in the hands of competent managers. The theory proves the point, but it is surprising that so few people are aware of this fundamental principle of hedge fund investing.

Despite the proven advantages of hedge fund investing, the idea did not really catch on for some time. Even by 1968 the US Securities and Exchange Commission (SEC) only recognised 140 such funds. The late 1960s saw strong bull markets world-wide, including the US. Unfortunately not every hedge fund manager had understood and followed Jones's doctrine to the full. Many managers realised that if they kept their shorts to a minimum, their performance would improve during this bull market. They thus broke the cardinal rule of hedge investing – they cut their protection against the downside risk. Effectively they became geared, long-only practitioners; a highly dangerous position. As a result many "low risk" hedge funds were transformed into high-risk ones very quickly. Investors were unaware of the risks managers were taking, and were shattered to see the speed at which losses accumulated in 1969. This led to a general disaffection with hedge funds, and their gradual contraction over the next few years as a bear market set in.

Despite this earlier demonstration of the dangers of failing to remain hedged, a similar event took place in 1994. Some managers, operating in the bond markets, geared up to imprudent levels and suffered appalling losses as the US government reversed its interest rate policy in the February, causing a sell-off in global bond markets. How history repeats itself.

Following the débâcle of the late 1960s and early 1970s, hedge funds gradually began to bounce back. The good ones continued to outperform conventional US mutual funds. During this period the likes of George Soros, Michael Steinhardt and Julian Robertson set up business. However it was only in the mid 1980s that the industry took off as new financial instruments allowed more interesting and complex strategies to evolve in bond and equity markets. In addition, managers started to look for opportunities overseas in Europe and the emerging markets. Owing to very inefficient pricing large and relatively low-risk returns were available. For example, in some of the emerging Far Eastern markets, shares of the subsidiaries of high quality Western conglomerates were trading on a P/E of 3 or 4 owing to lack of local knowledge and understanding of how to price equities. Indeed, in Indonesia today, the shares of BAT Indonesia trade on a P/E of 8 and a yield of 10%, and yet have produced earnings per share growth at a compound 25% over the past 5 years.

The lack of exposure to an equities culture is revealed by the story I was told by a multi-millionaire Indonesian gentleman. His father had been decorating a house many years ago and noticed that the walls were papered with colourful share certificates. In return for his labour, he shrewdly asked for the certificates, which he later sold for a fortune.

In recent years, many new strategies have evolved as the industry has divided into the macro and micro managers. Typically the macro managers who manage large amounts of money, such as George Soros, have gradually been forced to pursue major macro event strategies rather than more traditional stock related strategies. This has happened as a result of liquidity constraints. Conventional investment opportunities simply cannot handle the amount of money they wish to invest. These investors capitalise on events like the exit of Sterling from the ERM or the fall of the Yen, in mid 1995, from its dramatically overbought levels.

In contrast, the investment styles of the micro practitioners are more stock driven, and more like that of Jones. They will often specialise in quite narrow sectors of the stockmarket, where their focus helps them to gain an advantage over the generalists. We shall examine some of the strategies they pursue in a later chapter.

It is still surprising to think that although hedge funds were first devised nearly 50 years ago and offer intrinsically better potential risk and return characteristics than long only funds, they have fallen behind in the race to capture investors' money. They have been far and away surpassed by conventional unit trusts and other mutual funds. Certainly the reluctance of regulators to treat hedge funds as the equals of traditional co-mingled vehicles has been a major drawback, but the financial community delights in beating the system. On this occasion, it has not tried as hard as usual.

Perhaps the reason is more closely related to the

way the funds themselves work. Despite the theoretical advantages open to them, considerable skills are required to make them run successfully. It is difficult for many professional investors to come to terms with shorting stocks. A good hedge fund manager has to be a fine stock-picker on both the buy and sell sides. Further, from time to time, a manager's strategy may not be successful. Each manager tends to have a preferred investment style which may not work in all market conditions. If he is out of tune with his market, he could be underperforming on both long and short positions, and any gearing would exacerbate the problem. Strong nerves are required in these situations.

Funds chasing absolute returns, ie. real positive returns, hedge to keep the risk of losses in check and achieve a satisfactory return rather than necessarily aiming to beat the market. In roaring bull runs, hedge funds often lag badly behind long-only funds which have no downside risk protection in place, as witnessed in 1995.

According to Van Hedge Fund Advisors, Inc. in 1995 the VAN US Hedge Fund Index rose by 23.7% compared to a rise of 37.6% in the S&P 500 Index. In contrast in 1992 and 1993 when the S&P 500 rose a more modest 7.6% and 10.0% respectively the VAN US Hedge Fund Index rose by 17.2% and 24.9%.

In the final stages of a major market rise, the more risk-averse hedge managers leave the party and reduce their market exposure to perhaps 25% or less. In such a situation these hedge funds will not share so much in those last dangerous gains, and may not match investors' expectations. In some cases, this temporary underperformance may tempt managers to relax the hedging component of their portfolios with worrying consequences should a sudden sharp bear market strike, as it did in October 1987.

In Figure 1.2 below we show the cumulative performance of the VAN US Hedge Fund Index over the past 6 years compared to the S&P 500 and the average US equity mutual fund. This chart shows the smoothing effect on performance of hedge funds and also their long-term superior returns.

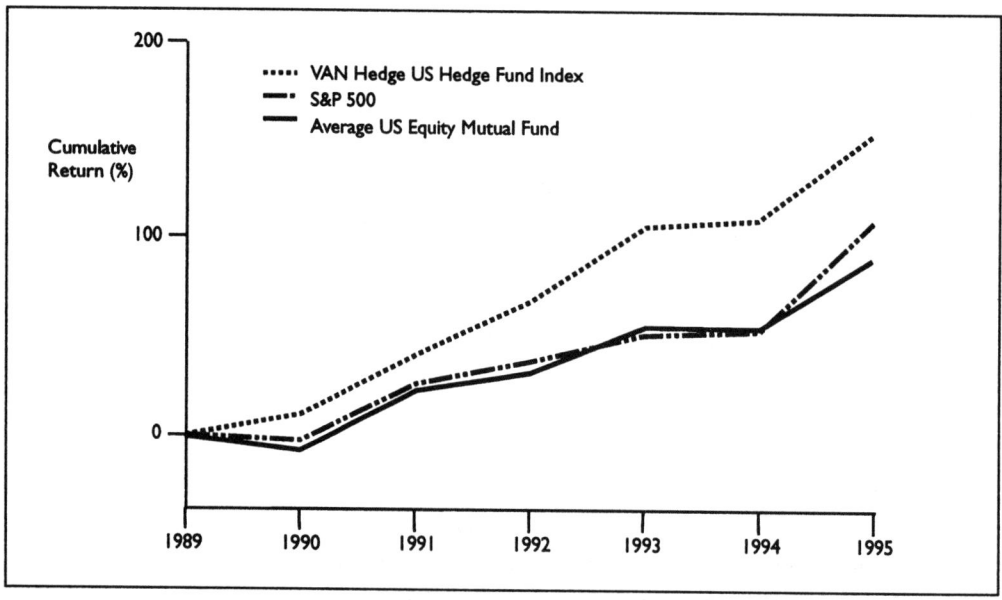

Figure 1.2 The cumulative return of the VAN US Hedge Fund Index compared to the S&P 500 Index and the Average US Equity Mutual Fund.

For now, the message is that hedge funds cover a wide spectrum of styles and risks. From the early days when the first fund was created to use gearing and short selling to increase returns but reduce risk, we have ended up with two new permutations. The first is the speculative geared fund, usually a futures fund. This strictly should not be considered as a hedge fund at all, since it does not control its risk sufficiently; although realistically it is too late to stop it from attracting the hedge fund tag. At the other end of the scale, there is the very low-risk fund. This uses hedging techniques extensively to reduce risk and produce returns little above the risk-free rate of return. Whilst perhaps all strategies are valid, they are not all suitable to the needs of individual investors. Caveat emptor.

Hedge funds have been much maligned by the press, and yet are barely understood. Unbalanced reporting has held back the acceptance of these funds in the UK. Many still consider hedge funds to be speculative, and for the high-risk investor only. Yet hedging and hedge funds are not new, nor are they all high risk.

The tide is turning. As more balanced articles appear and people become better informed about the diversification benefits of these funds they will earn themselves a place in conventional portfolios. Hedge fund risk/return characteristics are superior to those of conventional long-only funds. At the end of the day, if professional investors choose to ignore this, they risk underperforming their more open-minded peers. Performance will be the ultimate catalyst to changing perceptions.

2

SOME TYPICAL HEDGE FUND STRATEGIES

Thanks largely to George Soros, there is a great misconception about hedge fund strategies. Most investors tend to think that they all do the same thing – take some kind of giant bet on the outcome of macro-economic events. In reality, this is far from the truth. Hedge funds actually employ a vast array of strategies, ranging from the truly global macro-styles to the very narrow specialist ones which concentrate on a single aspect of a market, be it commodities, equities or bonds.

As we have seen in the opening chapter, hedge funds cannot be treated as an homogeneous group. Strategies vary widely, as do their risk profiles and performance attributes. In an equity market, the underlying shares represent companies carrying out very different types of business; so it is with hedge funds. Their strategies vary so much that the average investor would be hard pressed to see that they merely represent different points on the same compass.

Nevertheless, there are some recognised major styles which we have picked out below. Some funds may find themselves simultaneously in more than one "box", and over time their style may evolve to suit conditions. The most easily recognised style is the:

Global Macro Strategy – where the manager concentrates on understanding and predicting the outcome of macro-economic events in world markets. Often the manager concentrates on currency moves, and major interest rate realignments, and uses derivatives and leverage to take massive positions. The classic example was when George Soros went short of Sterling in September/October 1992. By selling short £10 billion and buying the position back for £9 billion, he pocketed £1 billion in the process. There were two crucial elements in spotting the opportunity for this coup. The first was recognising that Sterling could not stay in the ERM because it was fundamentally over-valued. The second was to appreciate that, on hearing that the UK's Chancellor of the Exchequer had borrowed £10 billion from the IMF to defend sterling, he had to short a similar amount of the currency before the British Government would run out of money.

Other Global Strategies break down as follows:

Global International – managers review world markets looking for opportunities, mainly at the stock picking level, to buy or short specific equities. This strategy also extends to shorting whole markets by using futures, and sometimes applying a currency overlay to hedge weak currencies into strong ones. A good example of this was employed by many managers in the summer of 1995. They went long of (bought) the Japanese Nikkei future, while shorting (selling) an equivalent amount of Yen for US$. The rationale here was that the Yen at around 80 to the US$ was dramatically overpriced. It had to fall or Japanese exports would hit a brick wall, resulting in economic catastrophe. Once it became obvious that the authorities were going to drive the Yen back up to around 100 against the US$, the currency became a one way bet and so did the market. The currency did meet its target, and the stockmarket recovered, although in the short term to a lesser extent than anticipated. The risk in this strategy was fairly low, but the rewards in 3 months were gains of over 30%.

Global Emerging Strategies – here managers invest in less mature markets where there are often large pricing anomalies. Take, for example, the situation in Russia following the breakup of the communist regime. The people were given vouchers or coupons, similar to shares, in a number of major companies. These vouchers were tradeable and could therefore be sold to third parties. A number of Coupon Funds were established, a little like UK investment trusts, where investors could exchange their coupons for shares in the fund and so diversify their investment. Owing to poor demand, over time the shares in the Coupon Funds moved to a discount to the underlying net asset value (NAV) of the fund, sometimes up to 50%. International investors bought large amounts of these vehicles at significant discounts to their NAV from disillusioned investors.

At the same time, by buying put options on the Russian market from international banks, they were able to protect their long position in the Coupon Funds against an unexpected market collapse. Once they had accumulated a large enough holding in a fund the international investors would approach the manager and threaten to take over the fund. In many cases the investor was bought off by the fund buying back his shares and cancelling them. In other cases the fund was taken over by outsiders and liquidated, producing large profits for the arbitrageur.

Discounts on investment funds are not rare and often occur in the UK but rarely to the same degree. It is also often more difficult to take over the management of such funds here compared to Eastern Europe.

The higher risks involved in emerging compared to mature markets are reflected in large potential gains for brave but careful investors. Markets in this category include the smaller South American, Asian and Eastern European stockmarkets. Generally most of the strategies are long in nature with a hedge (put options) applied, as demonstrated in the example above. In some markets it is not permissible to short stocks, although synthetic shorts can be bought through the major international broking houses.

Another good example of a Global Emerging Strategy was demonstrated in the second half of 1995 by Infinity Investors. They had noticed that Turkish Treasury Bills with 6 months to expiry were yielding 96%. Such a high return was anticipating a fall in the Government, general economic and political mayhem, and possibly a default on government debt. Infinity realised that a default on domestic debt was highly unlikely, since all a government has to do to service its debt is to print more money. Foreign denominated debt is the problem, because there you actually have to obtain the hard currency to pay interest, and if no one is willing to exchange the appropriate currency for your money you must default. In fact, with the exception of the Ivory Coast, no country has reneged on its domestic debt; and the Ivory Coast failed because its currency was underwritten by the French Government, and effectively linked to the French Franc. When the French withdrew their support, the Ivory Coast could not pay interest on its essentially French Franc debt.

Infinity were fairly certain that they would not lose their principal through a Turkish default. But given the parlous state of the country, a massive devaluation was expected, either through normal market forces, or as a result of direct action from the Government. Infinity therefore had to hedge out the currency risk, the most difficult part of the transaction. Unfortunately the foreign exchange market does not provide forward quotes for the US$:Turkish Lira, so some other means had to be found to forward hedge the Lira. A British merchant bank with connections in Turkey was contacted. This bank found a Turkish commercial bank which had a client who was willing to sell a US$:Lira put option with a 6 month duration and a strike price 50% below the current exchange rate. The British bank guaranteed the deal, which was agreed for a premium of 2% of the total contract price. The Turkish client would gain if the currency did not depreciate by more than around 50%, which seemed a good risk. Infinity gained because it could do a deal where previously it was unable to hedge out sufficient of the risk. The parameters of the deal for Infinity were:

	%
Yield on Turkish T-Bills	48 (96% pa.)
Cost of Put option	2
Maximum potential return	46

The maximum potential loss would occur if the Lira depreciated more than 50%, and would be equivalent to $50 - 46 = 4\%$ of the value of the Treasury bills bought.

On the upside, assuming the exchange rate did not change, the return would have been 46%. The risk/return ratio of this deal looks very good – minus 4% to plus 46%. The actual outcome was indeed good – a US$ profit of 20% in 6 months. This example illustrates the potential to make money in more esoteric transactions, but the difficulty of actually executing the deal should not be underestimated. Putting on the hedge was far from easy, and required contacts and patience. Such skills are not so readily available among more conventional investors.

Regional Specific Managers – these concentrate exclusively on one market or region, for instance the UK, or Europe. These managers are normally interested in stock selection strategies, going both long and short following the traditional Jones model. In the case of Europe, some managers offer to price their fund in US$ or another currency, often the DM. This means that they will hedge all underlying currency exposure, for instance Sterling and French Francs, into US$ or DM as appropriate. This undoubtedly adds to the attractions of the product for the international investor.

There are no trades which typically characterise a regional specific manager; the variety is so great. But to take a typical example of a transaction which could take place, look at Eurotunnel. Its revenues do not match its interest payments, and are unlikely ever to do so without further refinancing or government assistance. The perfect strategy here is to sell the stock short. The monies received from the sale can be put on deposit at 6%. Less say the 2% required to meet the cost of borrowing the stock which must be delivered, we are left with an annualised return of 4% for holding a short position in a company that should ultimately fail. Through buying a call option which is well out of the money, the right to buy shares at a set price for a given period, we can gain protection against most of the potential losses resulting from the UK Government helping the company and the share price unexpectedly rising.

Distressed Securities – is one of the two main examples of event-driven strategies; the other is risk arbitrage. The former concentrates on shares in companies which are being reorganised and/or are in bankruptcy. Studying the underlying assets in great depth, the investor forms a view on whether after the reorganisation or emergence from bankruptcy the shares will be worth more than their current price. Often more conservative investors shy away from such investments, perceiving them as high risk. To a degree this may be so but, if not too much of a portfolio is allocated to any one company, the overall risks can be much reduced.

The Risk Arbitrageur – this category follows many strategies, varying from low to high risk. Low-risk strategies could involve taking a view on future interest rates and, for instance, going long of short-dated bonds and short of long-dated issues. Here let us suppose that interest rates are going to fall. Generally bonds with the same coupon but different maturities will not behave quite in the same way. Both will see their yields drop as their prices rise but the bonds with the longer maturities will generally perform the best. This is because they are giving the investor the opportunity to lock into attractive yields for longer than short-dated bonds. This is worth paying a little extra for. Therefore in times of falling interest rates if you buy long bonds from the proceeds of selling short bonds, not only can you make the transaction almost self-financing, you should be able to take a small margin in the middle. And if the market turns against you, you will have some, albeit limited, protection from your short positions.

High-risk strategies cover a manager simultaneously buying stock in a company which has attracted a take-over or announced a potential merger, and selling the stock of the acquirer or merger partner. The downside to this transaction is if the bid/merger fails to go through. This can sometimes be large. For instance, in the Granada bid for Forte in late 1995, consider the case of the arbitrageur who bought Forte shares on the initial announcement of the bid and simultaneously sold Granada shares. Assuming that the investor waited until Friday, 19 January, just 3 business days before the last day for acceptance of the bid, to unwind his deals, then he would have made the following profit:

	£ COST/ (PROCEEDS)*	£ PROFIT/(LOSS)*
22 November 1995 – Take-over announced:		
– buys 200,000 Forte shares at 342p	(684,000)	
– sells 100,000 Granada shares at 654p	654,000	
19 January 1996 – Closes out previous deal:		
– sells 200,000 Forte shares at 373p	746,000	62,000
– buys 100,000 Granada shares at 690p	(690,000)	(36,000)
TOTAL PROFIT		£26,000

Excluding expenses

If, however, the manager went all the way to the wire and waited for the final vote on 24 January and Forte had retained its independence the price moves could have been very different. Forte shares would probably have fallen back to around 300p while Granada might have fallen to 630p, on the back of disappointment that it did not get its prey. The loss on this transaction would then have been £60,000.

Market Neutral Strategies – attempt to neutralise market risk to capture the "Alpha" of the portfolio, which is the non-systematic risk of the portfolio. Market neutral means that irrespective of whether the market rises or falls the impact on the investor's portfolio is irrelevant since his long positions match his short ones. He is purely looking for stock selection gains. This is achieved by constructing a portfolio consisting of two equal halves, one long and the other short. As the long positions gain in value relative to the stockmarket so the short positions fall more than the market, resulting in gains on both positions. The problem in reality is ensuring that both elements are representative of the market, otherwise they will not be hedging out market risk to the degree anticipated. Share selection and quantitative modelling is the key to this strategy, and only the best managers are able to produce consistently good returns. The most well-known "sub-sets" of this strategy are:

> **1. Convertible arbitrage** – the manager looks to capture anomalies between the price of the underlying shares and their convertible securities. Normally he goes long of the convertible, and short of the underlying shares. In theory, this is a very low-risk strategy, since the longs nearly balance the shorts in all but volatility. For example, consider the fictitious company Arox plc which has a convertible security, which converts into ordinary shares at a ratio of one to one and has a life to conversion of only one year.

- Share price 100p: dividends in next 12 months – 6p gross.

- Convertible price 95p: interest payments due in next 12 months – 6p gross.

Over the next 12 months assuming the stockmarket is static then the returns from these two investments will be:

- Shares – 6.0%: just the dividend income.

- Convertible – 11.3%: interest and the move up in the price to match the value of one ordinary share which will be received on conversion.

By going long of one convertible share and short one ordinary, over the course of the year you would expect to make: 11.3%–7.0% (cost of financing and transaction charges): in total perhaps 4%–5%. If this deal were executed in a transaction worth £1 million the profit would be of the order of £40,000–£50,000. The downside risk is very small. If the market collapses the convertible issue will fall less than the shares because its much higher yield will offer support.

2. Fixed-income arbitrage – the manager buys bonds, and sells short against them Treasury bonds of similar rate and maturity. Here again we are looking at the market mis-pricing securities, and the opportunity to benefit from this. This is very similar to the example shown under "The Risk Arbitrageur" (page 45) where we looked at long/short maturity arbitrage.

3. Hedged arbitrage – this is a strategy used not only by hedge fund operators but also by market-makers in integrated broking houses. Here the manager buys a basket of stocks which he thinks will rise against the market and sells short against them a stock index future. Of course the reverse trade may also occur where stock is sold short and a stock index future is purchased.

Suppose we buy a basket worth £10 million, consisting of the following shares in equal amounts by value and at the prices shown, and then sell them five weeks later, again at the prices shown:

	13/12/1995*	22/1/1996*	Change (%)
FT-SE 100 Index	3662.4	3754.2	2.5
BATS	571.0	578.0	1.2
Shell	843.0	845.0	0.2
GEC	320.0	359.0	12.2
Hanson Trust	192.5	206.0	7.0
BTR	343.0	379.0	10.5
Willis Corroon	141.5	151.0	6.7
*All share prices are in pence.			Average gain 6.3%

As we show on page 50 the stockmarket rose over the five week period quite strongly, by 91 points or 2.5%. The March FT-SE Index Future we sold to cover our long position in individual stocks actually rose slightly more than the stockmarket. This was because investors were expecting the market to go even higher and were prepared to pay a premium to buy the future.

	13/12/95	22/1/96	% Gain
FT-SE 100 Index	3662.4	3754.2	2.5
March FT-SE Index Future	3685.0	3780.0	2.6

Fortunately the shares we bought rose 6.3% more than the Index future and so a good profit was made on this transaction, of roughly £370,000.

Aggressive Growth Funds – the manager selects stocks from the high growth areas of the economy such as technology or biotechnology, then reduces risk by shorting positions using options. An example might consist of buying six shares which are all high risk but potentially high return and simultaneously purchasing put options 10% below the current share price, at a cost of 5% of the value of the share. If we assume the first two shares rise 50% over the next 6 months and the last four halve, we have still made a good profit owing to the downside cover put in place. If we had not bought put options we would have lost nearly 20% of our capital.

Share	Cost Price	Sale Price	Profit/(Loss) No option cover	Profit/(Loss) With put option cover
1	100	150	50	45
2	100	150	50	45
3	100	50	(50)	(15)
4	100	50	(50)	(15)
5	100	50	(50)	(15)
6	100	50	(50)	(15)
Totals	600	500	(100)	30

Market Timing – the manager essentially switches between "no load" mutual funds and cash. The manager pays no premium or charges for buying these no load funds. If he thinks the market will rise he buys into the funds and when he thinks the market will fall he sells again. Since he has no transaction costs this is a very efficient way of trading the market and using his skill to pick the exact time to buy and sell.

Several-Strategies – here there is not one strategy employed but a combination. This mix may well vary over time as market conditions alter. The manager is not constrained to use any particular skill based strategy. He will look for opportunities everywhere and if, for instance, he can see an arbitrage he will invest in it. Likewise if there is a situation where he can benefit from a global macro strategy he will. To a degree Soros falls into the several-strategies category although he makes most of his spectacular gains from global macro strategies.

Short-Selling – this is as simple as it seems. Shares are sold short in an attempt to outperform the market. This is a very difficult strategy in strong bull markets, but a useful tool in a bear market, where more traditional managers buy short-selling hedge funds to profit from the expected market fall. We have seen this example already in a hedged form with the sale of Eurotunnel shares (see page 44). In its unhedged form the shares are just sold, with no insurance policy in place via a call option, to cover a sudden price rise.

Yield Curve Trades – this is when the manager matches long/short bond positions at different points on the yield curve to benefit from an anticipated change in the shape of the yield curve. Risk can be limited by having no net exposure to the market, but not eliminated in pure terms. This was a good strategy in early 1995, when the US Federal Reserve Bank stopped raising interest rates and large gains were to be made in long maturities and relatively small gains in short maturities. As we have already seen on page 45, the investor merely sells short dated maturities and buys longer dated ones. At some point in the future he reverses this strategy to lock in his profit.

Fund of Funds – involves buying stakes in a variety of hedge funds. This allows investors access to the skills of a portfolio of managers, something they would not normally be able to achieve themselves because of the high minimum investment required by many funds. This style is excellent for those who wish to spread risk across a number of funds and want to know that the portfolio is being managed by professionals at all times.

HOW WELL DO THESE STRATEGIES PERFORM?

Though data on hedge funds is not as freely available as it is on unit trusts or US mutual funds, figures from Van Hedge Fund Advisors, Inc. give us a very good overview of what the major performance trends in the industry have been in recent years and specifically in 1995.

Van Hedge Fund Advisors, Inc. maintains what is believed to be the largest database of hedge funds in the world, monitoring the performance of approximately 1,500 hedge funds (900 US, 600 Offshore) that actively manage over US$80 billion in assets. Van Hedge Fund Advisors, Inc. works with the faculty of the Owen Graduate School of Management of Vanderbilt University in its hedge fund research.

According to George Van, Chairman of the Company, 1995 was a good year. In the following pages we have included a précis of the Company's 1995 report on the industry together with performance tables for the following:

VAN US Hedge Fund Indices

VAN Offshore Hedge Fund Indices

A SUMMARY OF THE VAN HEDGE FUND ADVISORS, INC. 1995 REPORT

Investors interested in long-term performance should note that in the eight years since the inception of the Van Hedge database, the average US hedge fund achieved a net compound annual return of 18.4% compared to net compound annual returns of 13.5% for the average equity mutual fund and 15.6% for the S&P 500.

Equally interesting is that, of the US hedge funds currently reporting to Van Hedge Fund Advisors, Inc. 51% have experienced no calendar year losses at all since their inception, through to 1995. By contrast, only a relatively small percentage of mutual funds have escaped losses over the years. In 1994, for example, as a single recent year, only 37% of US equity mutual funds were profitable. This should lay to rest the notion that hedge funds are inherently "high-risk" investment vehicles.

For 1995, hedge fund returns by investment style were as follows:

	US (%)	Offshore (%)
Aggressive Growth	36.0	25.4
Distressed Securities	17.6	16.2
Emerging Markets	1.0	−0.7
Fund of Funds	16.8	15.6
Income	13.8	6.8
Macro	13.3	7.9
Market Neutral Strategies-Arbitrage	17.4	n/a
Market Neutral Strategies-Hedged	19.2	n/a
Market Neutral Strategies	n/a	8.8
Market Timing	7.5	11.7
Opportunistic	28.4	23.5
Special Situations	22.2	19.7
Short-Selling	−10.5	−16.4
Several Strategies	22.0	n/a
Value	31.2	15.1

Source: Van Hedge Fund Advisors, Inc.

Figure 2.1 Hedge Fund returns in 1995 by investment style.

Sector-oriented US hedge funds, those that invest primarily in specific industries, were up sharply in 1995, ahead of the full-year performance of the S&P 500 and well ahead of the performance of the average US equity mutual fund or US hedge fund. Despite their hedge-dampened market positions, the average US hedge fund only slightly underperformed the average US equity mutual fund in 1995 and substantially outperformed Offshore hedge funds.

US sector hedge funds did exceptionally well in

1995, even when one factors in the substantial overall run-up in the stockmarket during the year. Van Hedge Advisors, Inc. track the performance of four sectors which they call Financial Services, Healthcare, Media/Communications and Technology. Collectively, these sector hedge funds returned 41.5% net on a money weighted average in 1995, ahead of the 37.6% gain recorded by the S&P 500 and well ahead of the 25.1% net returned by the average US equity mutual fund, the 15.0% returned by the average US bond fund, the 23.7% net returned by the average US hedge fund and the 10.0% net returned by the average Offshore hedge fund.

Individually, US sector hedge funds in 1995 performed as follows, according to Van Hedge Advisors, Inc.: Financial Services, up 45.6%; Healthcare, up 47.4%; Media/Communications, up 22.0%; and Technology, up 42.9%.

Despite all the hype surrounding the technology sector in 1995, excitement that was well founded until recently, it is interesting to note that Healthcare and Financial Services hedge fund sectors performed very well during the year and outperformed the Technology sector.

	Calendar Years						Net Compound Annual Return
	1990 %	1991 %	1992 %	1993 %	1994 %	1995 %	1990–1995 %
SECTOR PERFORMANCE							
Financial Services Sector	−13.1	26.9	31.3	33.1	8.3	45.6	20.3
Healthcare	n/a	60.0	17.7	30.0	−4.0	47.4	23.0
Media/Communications	−26.1	27.3	17.3	51.0	−10.9	22.0	10.6
Technology	14.6	41.6	12.8	13.6	6.7	42.9	21.2
Av. Sector Performance	−10.2	36.4	20.0	28.6	2.8	41.5	17.9
STYLE PERFORMANCE							
Aggressive Growth	2.9	47.8	18.1	22.0	0.4	36.0	19.7
Distressed Securities	6.6	38.4	26.7	31.3	2.7	17.6	19.8
Emerging Markets	27.5	43.4	27.6	75.5	−8.5	1.0	24.8
Fund of Funds	11.0	9.9	9.5	21.1	−1.2	16.8	11.0
Income	10.2	28.2	16.8	20.7	−0.8	13.8	14.1
Macro	12.4	39.9	18.1	45.9	−16.4	13.3	17.0
Market Neutral Strategies – Arbitrage	9.7	16.0	13.2	17.4	3.8	17.4	12.8
Market Neutral Strategies – Hedged	22.1	25.3	15.8	22.9	4.2	19.2	18.1
Market Timing	19.6	54.2	13.7	13.9	3.1	7.5	17.6
Opportunistic	3.2	43.3	26.3	31.3	3.8	28.4	21.8
Several Strategies	6.2	32.2	17.8	23.4	0.3	22.0	16.5
Short-Selling	37.3	−17.9	6.0	−5.1	13.7	−10.5	2.4
Special Situations	11.4	28.2	17.3	29.7	2.5	22.2	18.2
Value	−1.4	34.3	17.5	26.2	2.8	31.2	17.6
VAN US Hedge Fund Index	7.7	30.2	17.2	24.9	1.4	23.7	17.1
BENCHMARKS							
S&P 500	−3.1	30.3	7.6	10.0	1.4	37.6	13.1
Average Equity Mutual Fund	−6.9	32.0	6.6	19.4	−2.2	25.1	11.4
Average Bond Mutual Fund	7.8	14.6	6.1	8.4	−3.3	15.0	8.0
World Equity Index	−18.7	16.0	−7.1	20.4	3.4	18.7	6.5

Source: Van Hedge Fund Advisors, Inc.

Figure 2.2 VAN US Hedge Fund Indices 1990–1995.

| | Calendar Years | | | | | | Net Compound Annual Return |
	1990 %	1991 %	1992 %	1993 %	1994 %	1995 %	1990–1995 %
Aggressive Growth	1.9	42.4	13.2	28.5	–0.4	25.4	17.5
Distressed Securities	6.6	35.2	22.9	29.6	5.9	16.2	18.9
Emerging Markets	–10.4	26.5	21.8	86.3	–3.2	–0.7	16.3
Fund of Funds	14.9	17.7	14.3	29.1	–6.3	15.6	13.7
Income	14.5	22.1	12.4	22.3	–0.2	6.8	12.7
Macro	2.6	41.6	15.5	49.0	–11.6	7.9	15.6
Market Neutral Strategies*	8.9	19.8	16.7	20.7	1.3	8.8	12.5
Market Timing	9.2	31.2	9.0	28.8	–7.8	11.7	12.9
Opportunistic	4.2	55.6	28.9	31.7	0.5	23.5	22.7
Short-Selling	40.1	–23.4	10.9	–10.2	15.4	–16.4	0.5
Special Situations	11.8	30.9	17.6	26.7	5.7	19.7	18.4
Value	5.4	21.6	10.4	33.9	2.0	15.1	14.3
VAN Offshore Hedge Fund Index	6.0	28.0	16.8	37.0	–1.3	10.0	15.3
BENCHMARKS							
S&P 500	–3.1	30.3	7.6	10.0	1.4	37.6	13.1
World Equity Index	–18.7	16.0	–7.1	20.4	3.4	18.7	6.5

Source: Van Hedge Fund Advisors, Inc.

* The categories for Offshore funds do not always correspond to US funds due to differences in the databases.

Figure 2.3 VAN Offshore Hedge Fund Indices 1990–1995.

EXPLANATORY NOTES FROM VAN HEDGE FUND ADVISORS, INC.

- Past results are not necessarily indicative of future performance.

- All information provided for various managers or indices is from sources believed to be reliable. Data are not necessarily audited or independently verified.

- S&P 500 returns reflect the reinvestment of dividends; World Equity Index returns do not reflect the reinvestment of dividends.

- Information on US and Offshore hedge funds is based on a sample of funds in Van Hedge Fund Advisors, Inc.'s database and may not be representative of all hedge funds. Van Hedge Fund Advisors, Inc. makes every effort to provide accurate information on hedge funds but does not warrant its completeness or accuracy.

- The sector hedge funds are a subset of the total VAN US Hedge Fund Index. The performance and statistics of these funds are also reflected in the various styles, as appropriate.

- Different statistics may be based on different numbers of funds, for technical reasons.

- All single-year hedge fund averages represent simple averages, not dollar-weighted averages.

- All hedge fund returns reported are net of fees and performance allocations.

- In some cases, predecessor portfolios have been included in performance numbers where such portfolios met various tests.

- This material is not intended as an offer or solicitation for the purchase or sale of any financial instrument.

* * *

3

WHO ARE THE PLAYERS?

Perhaps because the hedge fund industry is so little understood, the men at the top appear to have legendary status. Somehow they are almost the masters of the universe, shadowy individuals playing with massive sums of money, moving in mysterious ways. George Soros is known as the man who, almost single-handed, pushed the United Kingdom out of the European Exchange Rate Mechanism. His actions forced Chancellor Norman Lamont to stand blinking in the spotlight to admit ERM defeat.

The Gordon Gekko character played by Michael Douglas in the film "Wall Street" gets mixed in, adding to the image of ruthless figures who can move markets at a whim. This is counter-balanced by the growing publicity for the Soros Foundation, and the way in which Soros has channelled massive amounts into good causes in Eastern Europe, helping advance ailing economies. Many in the industry have not been keen to court publicity, happier to concentrate on maximising returns to investors rather than to feed the publicity machine. They have no need for it. They do not need to sell their services to the crowd. Their reputations are built more quietly, their performance speaking for them, becoming known to a select crowd who have big money to invest. A few are flamboyant, with extravagant life-styles, but most are consumed by their business, concerned with what they do, anxious above all to get things right. These people are exceptionally talented and show considerable flair in comparison to the more traditional manager who adopts a more judgemental, conformist approach.

This chapter looks in depth at some of the well known managers and their investment styles, and introduces two largely unknown names who are representative of the growing collection of gifted operators in this exciting field. We have also included some sketches on less well known names you may come across as further background information.

Over the years a handful of names have kept appearing in the press, and to a large degree have influenced the general perception of hedge funds. George Soros and the Quantum Fund have become part of folklore, followed by Michael Steinhardt of Steinhardt Partners who retired at the end of 1995, Julian Robertson of Tiger Management and Louis Bacon of Moore Capital Management. They are the big guns. According to MAR/Hedge[2] at the end of 1994 these men and their organisations accounted for around US$23 billion out of a total of US$80 billion invested in hedge funds monitored by MAR/Hedge.

Looking at a breakdown of US hedge funds by size, distribution is very skewed. There are some 20 funds with assets of US$1 billion, and over 50 in the

2. A major US source of hedge fund data: see page 140.

US$100–999 million bracket. However the majority manage US$50 million or less, with many funds of US$10 million and under. Most of the smaller ones are virtually unknown, although many have excellent performance records. The number of funds being formed weekly is impossible to assess accurately but it is probably far higher than most commentators imagine.

GEORGE SOROS

No book on hedge funds would be complete without a section on George Soros, perhaps the doyen of the cult, the man who has almost become Mr Hedge. The Quantum Fund which he started in 1969 has become one of the most successful investments of all time. A thousand dollars invested at inception would now be worth over two million dollars including re-invested dividends. The fund, which is at the higher risk end of the spectrum, has traditionally used gearing and concentrated on Soros's great skill in reading the big events in world economics and having the guts to back his views.

Soros describes his philosophy as three dimensional in comparison to the usual two dimensional long-only funds. The fund's capital is the base which supports the three dimensional structure. The starting capital is used to buy stocks. Using this as collateral, loans are taken to buy more stocks to gear up. At the same time, and in the same way as Alfred Jones invested, the fund also short-sells shares it thinks will fall. Unlike Jones, who did not have the tools to do it at the time, the fund also takes positions in currencies and index futures, both long and short. Thus the structure builds from the bottom up:

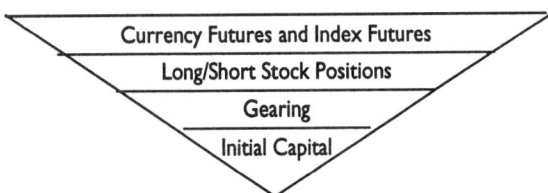

Currency Futures and Index Futures
Long/Short Stock Positions
Gearing
Initial Capital

Index futures are used to hedge and sometimes to gain market exposure, either on the long or short tack. Surprisingly, options are not used a great deal. Soros's rationale for this lies in the fact that the seller of the options is being paid to assume a different type of risk to that inherent in a geared portfolio. These two different types of risk do not match well enough to fit together intellectually in his three dimensional structure.

He has a highly developed and intuitive understanding of gearing. One of his tenets is that gearing is not simply how much you have borrowed on your capital, but a mix of this and the nature of the asset being geared. For instance, he points out that gearing ten to one on short dated bonds is not the equivalent of gearing ten to one on long dated bonds. Both are fixed interest securities, but they do not necessarily behave in the same manner because long dated bonds are much more volatile than short term instruments and therefore carry a much higher price risk.

Soros is an iconoclast when talking on modern investment theory. He does not believe that efficient market theories can provide the ultimate solutions to investment, because they only work most – not all – of the time. When the breakdown arrives, horrible results can occur. At that point there is no salvation in saying; "but the theory says..." He is more interested in the events which lead to these breakdowns, when most of the investment community is on the wrong foot trying to fit the outcome to the theory, rather than trying to profit from the inefficiency in the markets. In this complex world, he reduces everything to its lowest common denominator or benchmark against which he judges the value or otherwise of his investments.

Perhaps Soros's huge success comes down to his

assertion that he does not have a particular style. He is eclectic, and changes style to match conditions. Over the years, he claims his fund has changed its nature many times. In its first 10 years, it used no macro instruments while the last period of evolution has been dominated by them. More recently he has started investing in industrial assets, where he establishes ownership or part ownership of enterprises. But at all times the fund retains 20% of its assets for investment in macro strategies. Given the gearing possibilities, this does not inhibit him to any degree.

Undoubtedly Soros's skills are multiple and deep rooted. When starting a new strategy, he analyses the expected sequence of events, then compares them to the actual outcome. The intuitive ideal is therefore examined in a scientific framework. When he recognises that he may be wrong in his original thesis, his innate feel for risk gives rise to doubt and insecurity which drives him to act to remove the cause of this doubt. He claims he does this on two levels. He considers that his sense of his own fallibility is his strength, and uses this understanding to correct his errors. It seems that this reiterative process of constant appraisal and adjustment drives him on.

He also has an inner strength of self-belief. When he has developed a theory which is not immediately confirmed by the market, he will not sell merely because the market has not agreed with him, so long as his theory still stands up on rational analysis. If he believes his analysis is right, he is more likely to add to his position than to cut it. Of course, he is not always right. We all know about the 1992 "Black Wednesday" coup when the Quantum Fund made £1 billion on shorting Sterling, but he has also suffered some losses particularly in 1994 when the Yen proved stronger than anticipated. A similar situation occurred in early 1996.

Few men act in isolation; power is a lonely burden to bear. The Quantum Group is no longer one man, but a highly effective mix of like-minded individuals. Soros does not manage the investment side on a day-to-day basis, although he is closely in contact on all major strategies and always available to give advice. Today the fund is managed on a daily basis by Soros's lieutenants, who share a complementary relationship with the founder.

Despite Soros's great achievements, his life has not been a constant path to the stars. The history of Quantum's performance is not linear. Notwithstanding the 35% pa. compound growth from inception, the fund has seen distinct periods of success punctuated by intermittent flat spots. The early years of the 1990s were excellent, with strong gains in 1991, 1992 and 1993. But 1994 was the second worst year in the fund's history. Although it showed a profit, it was a modest 3%.

The fund was back on track again in 1995 with a return of 49.4%. This demonstrates the considerable skills employed by Soros and his team.

DR MARTIN ZWEIG

Dr Martin Zweig, a US based hedge fund manager, concentrates on shares, taking long and short positions. He is unquestionably one of the great all time long/short investors, regularly achieving excellent returns relative to his benchmarks. Not only has his performance been outstanding, but he achieves it with very low volatility, usually lower than that of the market itself. He keeps a keen eye on the risk in the market and if he feels it is low, he will be fully invested; if he considers it high, he will be quite liquid. And, as in 1987, when he felt the market risk was excessively high, he will be very short, using puts. In fact, on "Black Monday" in October 1987, his portfolio rose 9%, while the market fell 22.6%.

He tends not to make large bold moves, but prefers an incremental approach and finesses his moves. In neutral conditions, Zweig would be 65% invested and for a managed account his maximum and minimum positions would lie between 0% and 100%. Such extremes would unnerve the average mutual or unit trust fund manager. He generally would never be more than 20% liquid, arguing that investors have employed him to invest in stocks not cash. For a typical private partnership account, Zweig claims that he is always short, on average around 30%, and never less than 10%.

Absolute rather than relative gains are his goal. To protect portfolios ahead of falling markets he will short stock and sell index futures or options. He is more aggressive with managed funds than mutual funds, largely owing to tax regulations which reduce the flexibility of managing these types of funds. The decision to go liquid is difficult and success requires great nerve and skill. But Zweig does not look to capture major trends in their entirety. He is content to be 70% invested in a market rise of 20%, even if his portfolio only rises 15%. The risk of losing money is of far greater concern to him than the chance of making it. If the market fell 20% and he only fell 15%, he would nonetheless see this as complete failure.

Unlike Soros, who does not use extensive numerical analysis of previous relationships (quantitative analysis) to a great extent, Zweig is hooked on this approach. He employs a host of researchers to run correlations on all types of conceivable relationships; economic, fiscal, political – anything which may give an insight into how or why the market is performing as it is. He will test anything and keeps a completely open mind. He then enters the relationships which appear strongest into his model, weighting the closer correlations most heavily. Not surprisingly, the interest rate trend comes out on top. Interest rate trends tend to determine the direction of the markets. As rates rise, the markets normally falls. When they drop, the markets rise. The most recent example of this was in 1993 when falling global interest rates produced a huge global bull market.

Zweig will generally follow data back as far as he can. He cautions that market relationships change over time, and what used to work may not work so well today. His model's mix of variables is therefore constantly being adjusted. In his book *Winning on Wall Street*[3] he highlights the key variables as:

- Prime Rate
- Federal Reserve Discount Rate
- Federal Reserve, Reserve Requirements
- Money Supply
- Consumer Instalment Debt

The power of his modelling is quite staggering. Between 1954 and 1993, if you had followed his buy signals, you would have turned US$1,000 into US$33,999. This flies in the face of efficient market theory, supporting Soros's view that this theory only works some of the time. One reason why this may be so is that investors are not always looking objectively at hard numbers. Sentiment often takes over from fundamental analysis. To cover this Zweig also looks at the emotional levers such as the bullish/bearish sentiment of investment advisers.

3. Published by Warner (US). Available from Market Data Centre tel: 0171 522 0094.

He also looks at market factors such as:

The advance/decline ratio –
the number of shares rising divided by those
falling.

The moving average –
a series of plots which are the average of a number
of consecutive time periods. This results in the
smoothing of observed data.

New listings –
the number of new company listings on the stock
exchange.

For bear markets, his prime variables are:

Inflation versus deflation.
Price/earnings ratios for the Dow and S&P.
The yield curve.

He tends to weight monetary and interest rate
conditions quite heavily. He says he would like to attach
more importance to sentiment, but has difficulty finding
the right type of data. Actual price moves are not so helpful
since, although in a way they are the purest indicator of all,
they tend to have residual momentum. As a result, at the
top and the bottom of cycles, the signals will be going in
the wrong direction.

Zweig, like Soros, is obsessed with errors, but in a
different way. Soros seems to derive almost perverse
enjoyment in proving his fallibility, then recovering from
it. Zweig sees errors as failure, totally and utterly. He is
far more risk averse, conservative, careful, and concerned

about the possibility of losing money. Operating in the multi-dimensional global markets perhaps forces Soros towards a more expansive philosophy. Zweig sticks closely to his knitting.

JOHN W. HENRY

John W. Henry & Co. Inc. has over US$1.3 billion under management, and is the world's biggest pure futures trading adviser. In addition to its own direct accounts, it manages accounts for individual clients world-wide, including Merrill Lynch, Dean Witter and Smith Barney. Like Soros and Zweig, John Henry is a visionary. He founded the firm and leads the investment team. His claim to fame, apart from his superb long-term performance record, has been his ability to grow the business to such a size whilst continuing to achieve excellent performance.

Undoubtedly his investment style has been the key. It is based on systematic trend analysis but with a longer time horizon than the average operator. Typically Henry's positions are open for between 2 and 3 months. As a result, his turnover tends to be lower than that of the average manager.

His first investment programme was started in 1981, and invested in seven sectors. In 1988, the global diversified programme was opened. Although it trades the same sectors as the first programme, it uses a different quantitative model and only takes a position when a clear trend emerges. This programme has had over 60% up months, and a compound average annual return of over 27%. In 1992, the global financial programme was started, focusing on global currencies, interest rates, stock indices and energy. It follows long-term market trends rather than looking for short-term volatility. Since

1992, other strategies have been added. Now the firm has 10 programmes covering most financial and commodity markets.

JWH has one of the longest track records in the business and excellent performances. The annual compound rate of return for the company's funds is 24.7%. Despite the low turnover strategy, it has been suggested that the fund trades a massive 5% of the estimated US$25 billion plus invested in managed futures world-wide. Thus, size has not been a barrier to performance.

Henry's greatest achievement has been to develop the business while keeping the performance record intact. A feat that so many have failed to pull off. Does this success lie in the firm's positive attitude to growth? The managers actively welcome expansion, and see it as a constructive component of their long-term health. But managing it poses a great challenge at the operational and structural levels. All organisations must adapt as they grow larger. Traditionally, in fund management groups, the best investors have been elevated to the top management positions where they have then been let loose to manage its affairs with little or no formal training and often little innate ability. Buying and selling investments successfully is not the same as getting people to work as a team, or holding the various components of a company together in harmony. Not surprisingly results have often been poor since promotion also deprives the business of the individuals' investment talents.

The more successful groups in the UK – Mercury Asset Management plc, PDFM Limited and Schroder Investment Management Limited – have succeeded not through luck, but by adapting the company's structure skilfully as it has grown, and developing a strong corporate culture. Often along the way there have been problems, usually with people, but the strength of the organisation has overridden them.

The same is true of John W. Henry & Co. Inc. In 1989, Henry decided that the company had grown too large for him both to manage it and to run its investments. He stepped down from day-to-day management to concentrate on investment, and brought in a new president to run the company. The first step in the management of organisational change had been made. The new president lasted until 1993, and the second until July 1995. When he went, the company created an operating committee to focus on day-to-day decisions. The committee consists of five principals who all report to Henry and includes the managing director and the chief financial officer. With over 50 employees, the company is by no means small, but its concentration of senior personnel gives it a depth missing from many smaller companies.

As well as changing the organisation structure, Henry also made a fundamental adjustment to the risk profile of his funds. As with so many investment groups, the impetus for a change in investment style was related to a period of poor performance. You do not fix the engine before it's broken. In 1992 the financial and metals programme suffered a one month fall of nearly 40%. This was too much to bear. The problem lay with the success of previous months when the fund had recorded large gains. The stop losses had not been moved up closely enough behind the gains. When the fall finally came there was no protection.

Management took positive action to reduce volatility, and now concentrates heavily on monitoring all positions, and their inter-related volatilities. Their efforts have paid off. To date, downside risk has been reduced without dramatically impairing upside potential. For example, in the early years the financial and metals programme had standard deviations in the 75% to 200% range. Since 1993, these have been reduced to a range of 15% to 30%. The JWH risk-adjusted returns have also improved since 1992, and now appear towards the top of the charts. For the volatile financial and metals programme, the five largest monthly drawdowns (losses) have all been greater than 24%, but since 1992 there has been no loss greater than 17.5%. Compared to the opposition, JWH has also improved its relative record on the downside significantly. For example, the financial and metals programme's worst drawdowns in 1992 were 3.7 times as bad as the median of all managers, but in 1994/5 this had reduced to 1.7 times. On the other side of the coin, the upside potential has not been constrained. Since 1992 JWH has significantly beaten the median trend-following manager.

In 1995 strong gains were recorded across most programmes and volatility remained in check.

MONROE TROUT

Monroe Trout has a fantastic name, an excellent brain, and a stunning academic record. He can also make money. He is the intellectual trader and has written many notable papers on investment, and can legitimately claim to be a genius both in and out of the markets.

At 35, Trout is younger than the other managers mentioned so far. He is of the rocket scientist breed. He graduated from Harvard in 1984, magna cum laude, with a degree in economics. At Harvard he wrote six major papers on the forecasting of futures and options prices, and was generally reckoned one of the cleverest pupils of his time. Between 1984 and 1986, he worked for a proprietary trading firm in New York, NCZ Commodities, trading futures and options for the house and his own account. At the relatively early age of 24, he formed his own trading company.

The strategies he employs rely mainly on technical analysis, although he may look at fundamental analysis from time to time. Technical analysis is based on the notion that a study of market variables ie. volume, market volatility and open interest, will provide a means of predicting future prices. Fundamental analysis is more concerned with underlying business factors as a means of predicting future prices.

Trout uses a computerised statistical approach based on his own large database of prices, volumes, open interest, and other market statistics to develop and monitor trading strategies. This has allowed him to devise his own computer trading programmes and search for patterns which can be exploited. These underlying patterns are augmented by his experience and trading judgement. He tries to combine a rigorous scientific and intuitive approach to his decision making. Investment strategies can be changed at any time as new variables are introduced into the equation. Sometimes the messages from the quantitative system are overridden and the team may decide not to trade a given strategy. This intuitive component can influence outcomes significantly.

Trout currently monitors and trades over 150 commodity and securities markets, although not always continuously. On average, the company holds positions in half of the markets it analyses. Many of the instruments traded are geared, so the company often has a significantly greater position than its underlying net worth.

Making money is one thing but what makes Trout so exceptional is his risk-adjusted returns. His average annual returns are bettered only by a few, and his drawdowns by even fewer. His returns and the low level of risk taken to achieve them is unparalleled. Over the past five years, Trout Trading has achieved an annual return of some 67%, but his largest drawdown in this period was only about 8%. When it comes to consistency, he is up a staggering 87% of the time on a monthly basis.

Studying how he defines success gives a good insight into his own achievements. Trout believes that the investor with the best Sharpe Ratio[4] at the end of the period is the best trader. Put simply this means the investor showing the best risk adjusted returns.

Trout aims to make 30% pa., with no peak to valley trough (the fall from a high point to the next low point), greater than 10%. Such a high expected rate of return with low downside risk is incredible. Trout believes this performance is related to a combination of factors. Surprisingly Trout's typical holding period for a trade ranges between one day and a week. Yet, by his own admission, most trading models that generate very short term trading signals, of less than a week's duration, cannot beat the transaction costs.

How does he do it? Two things distinguish his trading profile from that of other short-term operators and allow him to beat the odds. His system is more statistically based and he achieves incredibly low transaction costs. Having several hundred million dollars under management and with very high trading turnover means that Trout trades more contracts than almost anyone. That gives him the clout to get the lowest cost and best

4. The Sharpe Ratio is explained fully on pages 119–121.

executions. Lowest cost relates to the commission charged by brokers for executing trades on the market floor; the more business you do with a broker the less he generally charges you per deal. Best execution consists of two variables; the size of the transaction and the price at which it can all be executed. When trying to complete a big deal it is sometimes better to give a little on price to do the business in one go rather than doing half now and leaving the balance. Often, before the balance of the order can be completed, the price has moved against you. Best execution relies on the broker using his skills to determine how he should execute the transaction to get the best terms for his client. Trout monitors his cost of transactions closely to ensure that the ongoing performance is the best that can be achieved. Good execution and a good statistical system, however, cannot be the whole answer to his success. At the end of the day he is actually very good at market timing. This skill probably creates at least half his returns and his low volatility.

His intuitive feel for risk is also reflected in his trading systems. They are designed to counter the sudden unexpected event which can shatter a highly geared futures strategy. As an academic, he is admirably placed to understand risk from the mathematical standpoint, and it is refreshing that he does not believe in the traditional efficient market theory. Rather, he contends that markets are neither always bound to follow the random walk hypothesis, where price moves from one day to the next are considered to be random, nor are they efficient. If they were, he would not have been able to achieve his outstanding risk-adjusted returns. Since he understands the shortcomings of **Modern Portfolio Theory**[5] better than

5. This is explained fully in Chapter 4.

most he is aware that the effect of rogue price moves is underestimated by conventional models, so risk control is essential. No wonder his risk return figures are so good.

INFINITY INVESTORS

Infinity Investors is based in Texas, and ranks among the most interesting of the up-and-coming groups. It seeks investment opportunities around the world, and has an excellent track record, with a good feel for risk control. One of the pleasant features of the fund is that the principal investment managers, Barrett Wissman and Clark Hunt, are both down-to-earth individuals who would not be out of place on the trustee board of a UK pension fund. Both have experience on Wall Street, on the corporate finance side rather than in direct investing, and both have had experience actually managing real companies.

Infinity is very entrepreneurial, yet it is managed as a true hedge fund. There is as much concern with downside risk as upside potential. Each trade is quantified in these terms. Only when the risk/return parameters are met is the investment made. Risk averse strategies with low market correlations – ie. where the outcome of the strategy, good or bad, has little to do with the underlying market – are the guiding tenets. Investments are made in a wide range of assets where the managers see good potential for significant yield, or capital appreciation, or both. Investments are made on a global basis, usually in marketable securities. If they feel there are insufficient opportunities at any given time, the managers will hold cash.

No more than 10% of the fund's capital is ever committed to any one investment, except cash. Great efforts are made to reduce the correlation between individual trades, so as to keep the overall risk level in the portfolio as low as possible. As a further attempt to reduce risk, hedging transactions are often undertaken to iron out fluctuations in interest rates, currency exchange rates and general economic conditions. Gearing is limited to twice capital.

One of the attractions of this fund is the esoteric nature of some of its investments. There have been a number of investments in managed currencies. Such currencies, like the Thai Baht, the Ecu, the Argentine Peso, and the Saudi Riyal, are not allowed to float freely, and are usually linked to a basket of currencies or to one individual currency. Because they trade at a fixed exchange rate, significant opportunities exist to benefit from the inefficiencies associated with these managed markets.

A number of strategies can be used to exploit them: examples include:

- The simultaneous purchase of money market instruments in the managed currency and the purchase of OTC (Over The Counter ie. not traded on an exchange) options from investment houses or industrial corporations to hedge the catastrophic risk of a change in currency policy.

- The outright purchase of money market instruments in managed currencies, where Infinity is able to lay off the risk of currency devaluation to a third party, or where the trade is executed and completed within a short time span.

- The trading of OTC options on managed currencies where Infinity is able to take advantage of mis-pricing in the market between investment banks and industrial companies. This is often caused by differences of opinion on volatility assumptions and lack of liquidity in such inefficient markets.

As an additional risk control measure, the manager does not usually invest directly in the money markets of managed currencies. Usually the transaction is "wrapped" by an investment bank, so that the fund does not bear the direct risk of illiquidity or exchange control risk.

Another major strategy employs discounted equity securities and equity arbitrage. Here the fund enters into a transaction where it buys equity at a discount to the market price. At present in the US many small and medium sized listed companies are hungry for cash to use for expansion. Sometimes they need this money quickly and cannot afford to go through the rigmarole of raising it directly from the stockmarket. Instead they opt to raise funds by what is called a *Reg S* deal. Here the company finds an investor who is prepared to take new shares in exchange for immediate cash. These new shares often have restrictions attached to them; for instance they normally cannot be sold for a certain period after receipt. In return for quick cash and acceptance of these dealing restrictions the company issues the shares at a steep discount to their market price.

Often, in order to improve returns or reduce volatility on these deals, Infinity uses a combined strategy of writing calls on the underlying security and buying puts on the same security or a related security or index. For example:

Infinity buys 1,000 shares of Mega Corporation in a Reg S deal for US$1,000 each. The market price is US$1,200.

It wants to protect itself against a market fall and/or a large fall in Mega Corporation shares while it is restricted from selling the shares in the stockmarket. And so:

It writes a one month call on 1,000 Mega shares at a strike price of US$1,200 and receives (say) US$10 per share (US$10,000). It has, therefore, sold the right to another investor to buy the Mega shares from it at a price of US$1,200 per share for a period of one month. From the proceeds of the sale of these calls it will now purchase downside protection.

It buys puts on Mega Corporation at a strike price of US$1,100 for US$20 per share. If the share price now falls below US$1,100 it knows it can sell all its holding at this price.

Therefore, if over the next month the share price rises above US$1,200, the shares will be called from Infinity but it will make a profit of US$1,200–1,000 – 10= 190 per share.

If, however, the price is X and lies between US$1,100 and US$1,200 the profit will be US$X–1,000–10 per share.

And if the price is below US$1,100 the put will be exercised and the return will be US$1,100–1,000–10=90 per share.

The minimum profit per share will be US$90 and the maximum US$190 but the probable outcome will lie somewhere in between. In this way Infinity has guaranteed a healthy profit irrespective of what happens during the period when it cannot sell.

The fund also invests in many types of bonds of any class, rating or currency. For example:

Sovereign Loans. These are loans to sovereign governments by financial institutions and were generally created in the 1980s with a floating rate of interest. They are traded in the international OTC secondary markets. They often feature high current yields and offer good capital appreciation prospects if the sovereign risk is considered to be improving.

Brady Bonds. These bonds were named after the former US Treasury Secretary Nicholas Brady. He was responsible for the setting up and management of a framework to coordinate a reduction in sovereign debt. Brady Bonds are securities created through a debt exchange of existing commercial bank loans, sovereign and private sector debts for new bonds. Many of these bonds are supported by investment grade assets which act as collateral for interest payments and capital.

Most Brady Bonds are in the name of Polish and Argentinian state entities. There is a flourishing secondary debt market, of which the Brady Bonds are a small subsection, and fortunes have been made trading the outstanding debt of such entities as the Vnesheconombank – the Bank for Foreign Trade of the USSR (a country which no longer exists). Merrill Lynch were buying Vnesheconombank debt at US$28 in early 1994 – the price rose by the end of that year to nearly US$50.

Pre-Brady Bonds. These are similar to the above but originated out of previous debt reduction programmes.

Domestic Debt. These are securities denominated in local currency or sometimes in US$, where the primary markets are the local market in which the security is domiciled.

Mexican Cetes are peso-denominated Mexican Government treasury bills that are auctioned weekly. The Argentine Bote is an example of a US$ denominated local instrument.

The Infinity investment programme is particularly interesting because of the way it uses financial institutions to create structured products and indexed securities. Access to some markets and strategies would not be possible by relying solely on conventional techniques. Products may include credit notes whose returns are based on the performance of an index, a basket of investments or even a single investment. The institutions are able to devise these products by hedging and balancing risks already on their books.

The value of relationships with these institutions cannot be overestimated. They help Infinity provide excellent risk-adjusted returns by providing the products to facilitate deals. Examining Infinity's approach gives you some idea of the thought involved in devising trading strategies, and illustrates how different this team is from the conventional long-only investment manager. Infinity is one of the new breed of smart investors with the ability to make lateral jumps to provide strategies for their clients, and with the connections to execute such trades.

EGERTON

Egerton is another promising new management group, notable because it marries proven stock-picking ability with a range of futures and options strategies. It is partly, but not quite all, British. The two principals are John Armitage, who was previously a top European fund manager with Morgan Grenfell, and William Bollinger, an American. Based in London, this team has grown funds under management rapidly, reflecting a very successful debut in hedge fund management. It now looks after over US$350 million. Egerton manages two offshore European funds which are essentially identical, apart from one being denominated in US$, and the other in DM.

The funds are managed in a traditional Alfred Jones manner, with long positions offset by shorts although the funds are normally run net long. The skill of the principals lies in share selection, an area where Armitage built a considerable reputation in his earlier career. Each country in Europe may be represented, with a net long, short or neutral position. The portfolio may also be net invested long or short. The managers use futures and options to aid flexibility.

The style is straightforward, but the most interesting thing to note is the improvement in performance since the managers moved from the confines of long-only investing to hedge investing. In Figure 3.1, below, we show Armitage's performance in the old and new environment:

PERIOD	John Armitage %	FT/S&P – Actuaries Europe Index %	Egerton Gross Returns %	Egerton Net Returns* %
April 1991– March 1994	26.8	17.8	—	—
December 1994 – December 1995	—	18.9	44.5	35.6
*Net of 1% Management Fee and 20% Performance Fee.				

Figure 3.1 John Armitage's investment performance as the manager of the Morgan Grenfell European Trust and as joint manager of the Egerton European Fund.

The comparison is enlightening. In the old form, he was an exceptionally good manager. In the new form he is even better. This shows how powerful a tool long/short investing can be in the right hands. The added armoury of weapons improves flexibility and aids superior returns while reducing risk. For example, if Egerton does not like a sector or country, it will not hold it. The conventional manager is unlikely to be so bold. And the ability to short stock has added real value. As an example, the fund started shorting Eurotunnel in early 1995 at around FFr17. The shares finished the year at under FFr7. The fund has benefited from this position not only with a paper profit, but also because it has had the monies raised from the sale of Eurotunnel shares available to invest elsewhere.

At the beginning of 1996, Egerton closed their fund to new subscriptions for a minimum of six months. This was after raising over US$350 million in just over 12 months since inception in late 1994. During this period, the US$ denominated shares rose by 35.7%, after all expenses, compared to a rise of 19.4% in the FT/S&P – Actuaries Europe Index (in US$) and a return of 14.7% for the average offshore European unit trust (source: Statswise). Compared to other funds the Egerton fund would have been placed 3rd out of 148 funds in its sector.

Soros, Zweig, John W. Henry, Monroe Trout, Infinity and Egerton mix some of the best-known and best-established names with some of the brighter newcomers in the hedge fund industry. They are just a few in a long and ever-evolving list. New stars are emerging regularly as individual managers leave established funds to start on their own, and old names fade. One or two have simply got it wrong, and gone out of business, like David Askin of Askin Capital Management, who cost investors most of his fund's US$600 million when prices of collateralised mortgage obligations slumped. Some long-established managers have been scaling down, returning cash to investors as they have found it harder to move enormous sums in and out of limited markets as freely as they would wish. Even Soros wrote to investors in July 1995 to talk about refocusing investment strategy, and emphasising investment in infrastructure projects in some funds, holding out the hope of good profits from longer term financing.

A brief selection of some of the more interesting names who are either retiring or emerging includes:

MICHAEL STEINHARDT

Michael Steinhardt is one of the hedge fund legends, a former Wall Street research assistant and one-time financial journalist who started an investment firm in 1967. Employing numerous traders and analysts, he always made it clear that he would make the ultimate decision on any position. A tough taskmaster, driving his staff from a desk shaped like the bow of a ship, he achieved a remarkably consistent performance over the long term.

It came as a shock when he took a hammering in 1994. His funds lost 28%, or over US$1 billion, hit by the crash in world bond markets and the slide in the dollar. He bounced straight back in 1995, with a gain of 23%. He claimed an average cumulative return of more than 30% a year for 28 years, against a US stock average return of 10.8%.

Like Soros and Zweig, he has paid keen attention to errors, pointing to the importance of balancing the conviction to follow ideas and the flexibility to recognise mistakes. He has adopted a variety of trading approaches, including long and short-term market timing, stock selection and analysing sectors. He is keen on the contrarian approach, ready to take and hold on to large positions against the market when an opportunity arises.

Late in 1995, he announced that he was going to withdraw from the business, though he was running some US$4 billion of funds. At the age of 54, he vowed he was going to return cash to his investors. In a letter he spoke of the intensity required to manage funds, and the tremendous commitment required to do it well. He is talking of devoting more time to political and Jewish educational causes.

JULIAN ROBERTSON

Along with Steinhardt, Julian Robertson is one of the hedge fund giants, running some US$8 billion with his Tiger and Jaguar funds. For 1993, Tiger scored a return of 61%. He had a losing year in 1994, but his funds hit all-time peaks in 1995, rising more than 14% in the year. In his mid-sixties, he claims that his team of almost 200 has the highest ratio of talent to assets in the business, and believes that size is no obstacle to success. In 1995, he set about raising US$1 billion for a venture capital fund which would carry a five year lock-up with the aim of exploiting illiquid opportunities around the world.

PAUL TUDOR JONES

Like Michael Steinhardt, Paul Tudor Jones has been scaling down. He reduced his funds under management by a third, giving back US$670 million to investors in 1994, worrying about the difficulty of maintaining performance when handling large sums.

When the stockmarket crashed in October 1987, the Tudor Futures Fund achieved a 62% return. He says he had been expecting a crash, thanks to a model which picked up the correlation between the 1920s and the 1980s markets. Starting as a broker, he went on to score remarkable gains as a floor trader on the New York Cotton Exchange, then moved into money management in 1984. Press coverage builds on his flamboyant image, with talk of fine homes, and a private 3,000 acre wildlife preserve, but he has also been involved in supporting organisations to help the poor. A contrarian trader, he emphasises the dangers of losing money as opposed to making it. Heavily into risk control, he uses stop loss positions based on time and price, cutting exposure as positions move against him.

BRUCE KOVNER

Bruce Kovner, head of Caxton Corporation, taught political science at Harvard, toyed with politics, then decided on a career change. He spent a year studying markets and economic theory, and devoted particular attention to interest rates. After trades on his own account, he moved into commodities trading. Caxton made a return of more than 30% pa. net to investors in the first 12 years, faltering in 1994.

In June 1995, he returned US$1.2 billion, or two-thirds of the money he managed, to investors. He said that US$2 billion of capital was too unwieldy. He cut staff and moved to a smaller capital base in an effort to return to higher profitability. He follows a wide-ranging mix of international fundamental and technical analysis, with a strong emphasis on risk management, deciding on an exit point before he enters a trade. He is keen to assess risk over the whole portfolio, allocating wider stop losses to a smaller number of trades in preference to tight stop losses on numerous contracts.

DAVID WEILL

David Weill is the hedge fund ace who did not bounce back. Running US$1.2 billion, he scored a return of 63% in 1993 for his fund management company Vairocana, (apparently Sanskrit for "the great conqueror"). An American in his mid-thirties, with a keen interest in Buddhism, he came undone in 1994, losing US$700 million in a matter of months. Operating with a small staff, in a mansion overlooking St James's Park in London, he took a substantial position geared to a fall in European interest rates. Huge positions in English and German bonds were mixed in a complex tangle which caused difficulties in producing ready valuations. He attracted funds on the strength of support from a leading London banker and investment manager, who was considerably embarrassed when the funds repaid backers and closed. Weill left, making it known that he intended to visit ashrams in India.

CRISPIN ODEY

Crispin Odey hit the headlines in the UK when he enjoyed a £19 million pay packet for his hedge fund skills. He was paid in 1994 on the strength of a brilliant year in 1993. But in 1994 he lost £400 million from his funds, half as investors pulled cash out, the rest from trading losses. Towards the end of 1995, he was staging something of a recovery.

NICK RODITI

Nick Roditi has emerged as one of the stars of the Quantum empire controlled by George Soros, thanks to the rapid growth of the Quantum Quota Fund in which he manages the largest chunk of assets. Quota rose 140% in 1995. In his late forties, he worked at Schroder, then in Lord Rothschild's stable at RIT Capital. He was born in

Zimbabwe, and splits his time between Africa and Europe. His special talent is in predicting interest rate moves, and playing currencies, gearing up to make the most of such moves.

RAJ RAJARATNAM

Manager of the Needham Emerging Growth International Fund, Raj Rajaratnam was running with growth of more than 50% for the third quarter of 1995 and approximately 70% by the year end, chasing undervalued growth companies. Many investors in the fund were linked to technology companies, and Needham & Company was able to draw on its strong connections.

JAMES BENNETT

Highly successful as a manager at Sega Associates, James Bennett specialises in troubled companies and special situations at Bennett Management. He devotes great effort to analysing the underlying value of out-of-favour companies which have emerged from financial restructuring.

His fund has one of the most consistent returns and best Sharpe Ratio around.

At the end of the day, successful money management is not down to just one factor – a system, good people, low execution costs; it is an amalgam of these and other things. The approach of managers varies considerably, along with their temperaments. All need flair and sound instincts and, above all, must follow disciplined trading rules.

The winners do not make money by luck. They are the Olympians of the money making managers, the skill players.

* * *

THE NEW WORLD – POST MODERN PORTFOLIO THEORY

Historically investors have tended to concentrate on expected future returns when selecting investments. Risk has been less of a consideration. This was partly because there was no adequate method of measuring it. Recently, however, there has been a breakthrough in investment theory with the transition from **Modern Portfolio Theory** to **Post Modern Portfolio Theory.** A fuller understanding of risk now allows investors to appreciate the benefits offered by hedge funds and the way in which, if used properly, they can help to control risk.

Modern Portfolio Theory was devised nearly 50 years ago, largely by Harry Markowitz, to help explain the relationship between risk and return and to develop a methodology to find the most efficient portfolio using a mix of assets. The model works theoretically, but from the beginning it was known to have shortcomings and in certain cases produced counter-intuitive results. As a consequence, and with the use of more advanced statistics and more powerful computers, a new approach has been developed. This is based on the original and is called **Post Modern Portfolio Theory.** This now forms the backbone of leading edge money management strategies and has revolutionised our views on what are risky assets and what are not.

In the 60 years to the end of 1995 gilts, according to the January 1996 BZW Equity-Gilt Study, have produced no gains in real purchasing power. They have been a disastrous investment. **Modern Portfolio Theory,** however, would still categorise gilts as low risk investments over the period because their standard deviation of return has been much less than equities. In addition, this theory would suggest that you should always hold a reasonable weighting of this asset in a low risk/low return portfolio. **Post Modern Portfolio Theory** does not agree and would classify gilts as a high risk investment over this period because they have produced no real appreciation in value. Intuitively this is not difficult to understand. It is this basic difference in the definition of risk which separates the two theories.

Risk when defined in terms of standard deviation is a measure of how much returns vary over a period compared to the longer term underlying trend. It is therefore a measure of dispersion and the equation we use to measure it is as follows:

$$\sigma = \sqrt{\frac{\sum(x-\bar{x})^2}{n}}$$

where: σ = the standard deviation
x = performance over each segment of the period, perhaps a month
$\bar{x}$ = the average performance of a segment over the whole period, perhaps a year
n = total number of segments

Example

Compare two investments A and B. During the course of a year, both rise by 2% per month. When their standard deviations are calculated we find that for A it is 25% of the mean monthly rise or 0.5, while for B it is 5% or 0.1. This means that A's results vary more widely than B's. We can predict from statistical theory that if relationships remain constant then approximately 68% of A's monthly rises will lie between 1.5% and 2.5%, and 68% of B's rises will be between 1.9% and 2.1%. Although we are uncertain how much A will rise next month compared to B, what we can say is that A shows more dispersion and is the riskier of the two investments.

How does **Post Modern Portfolio Theory** measure risk? First it starts from the premise that there is a risk-free rate of return, that is a rate of return which can be achieved with no fear of losing capital. This generally equates to the yield on short-dated gilts in the UK and Treasury Bills in the US. Over the long term since this yield is normally the same as or slightly above the rate of inflation, to maintain the real purchasing power of money, investments must at least match this figure. **Post Modern Portfolio Theory** therefore classifies gilts as high-risk investments over the past 60 years since, although over short-term periods they have offered good real returns, over the long term they have only achieved the basic minimum acceptable return. For this reason they would be excluded from any optimised **Post Modern Portfolio Theory** portfolio, and replaced by an asset which can exceed the minimum performance level even if its standard deviation or dispersion of returns is higher than gilts.

One small problem here is that, although over the long term gilt returns have been poor, their real returns vary according to the inflation outlook. Gilts actually offer quite good real risk adjusted returns during deflationary times and it is generally only during periods of rising inflation that their returns are poor. The investor must have a view on the likely rate of inflation to his investment horizon if he is to benefit from using the full powers of **Post Modern Portfolio Theory.** The further out the investor is prepared to look the more powerful the theory becomes as it smooths the impact of short-term behaviour from long-term trends.

MODERN PORTFOLIO THEORY

Modern Portfolio Theory assumes that investors want the least possible dispersion of returns for a given level of gain. It provides a methodology for selecting a portfolio of assets which is less risky than investing in any one particular asset. The theory views risk only as a function of dispersion.

In most situations, if you collect data that is influenced by many independent forces, it describes a bell shape when plotted as a chart. This is the normal distribution, and is also known as the Gaussian curve after its discoverer, the mathematician Gauss. Many natural phenomena conform to this shape, for instance, the height or IQs of people in a population. If you know the mean and the standard deviation (or variance) of the data, you can define the curve and draw it. This type of analysis is often referred to as mean-variance where variance is the name given to the square of the standard deviation, ie. variance = σ^2. It is important and useful because variances can be added. For instance, if two distributions had variances of σi^2 and σii^2 respectively, the variance of the two distributions combined would be $\sigma i^2 + \sigma ii^2$. Since only two variables are needed to define the curve, mathematically it can be worked on with relative ease.

There are some very important characteristics associated with the normal curve, as shown in Figure 4.1 on page 96.

- A vertical point drawn at the highest point of the curve marks the mid-point of the distribution and therefore 50% of the sample lies on one side and 50% on the other.

- Almost 100% of the distribution lies within three standard deviations of either side of the mid-point.

- 95% of the distribution is within two standard deviations either side of the mid-point.

- 68% of the distribution is within one standard deviation either side of the mid-point.

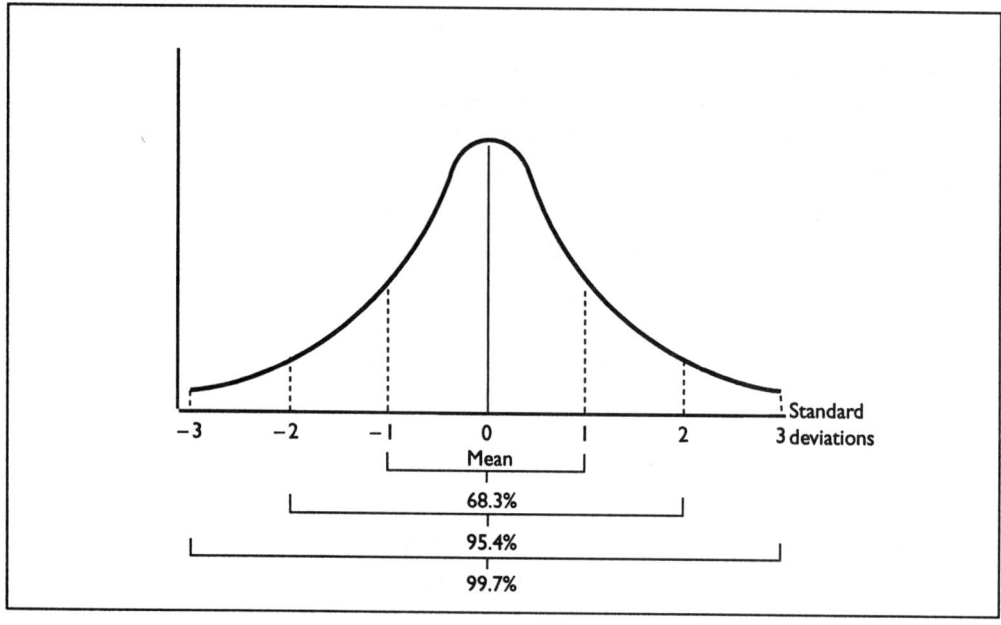

Figure 4.1 The Normal Curve

The mean corresponds to the average rate of return of the asset and the standard deviation, the variability of returns over time. **Modern Portfolio Theory** is based on the notion that over the long term any asset type will exhibit a relationship as described by the normal curve between its return and the variability of that return.

As stated before, the higher the dispersion risk, the higher the expected rate of return. Figure 4.2, on page 97, shows the results of a US study comparing the performance of stocks with other types of investments. The extreme right hand column shows a histogram of returns and graphically illustrates what is meant by dispersion risk. The dispersion for common stocks and small capitalisation stocks is far wider than for bonds or

US Treasury Bills, showing that these stocks are more volatile. The annual geometric mean rate of return column shows how the returns correlate to dispersion risk. There is clearly a very strong relationship between dispersion risk and return, and it is this relationship which forms the backbone of **Modern Portfolio Theory.**

Series	Annual geometric mean rate of return %	Highest annual return (and year) %	Lowest annual return (and year) %	Standard deviation of annual returns	Dispersion
Common stocks	10.0	54.0 (1933)	−43.3 (1931)	20.9	
Small company stocks	12.3	142.9 (1933)	−49.8 (1931)	35.6	
Long-term corporate bonds	5.0	43.8 (1982)	−8.1 (1969)	8.4	
US Treasury bills	3.5	14.7 (1981)	0.0 (1940)	3.3	
Consumer price index	3.1	18.2 (1946)	−10.3 (1932)	4.8	
					−50% 0% 50%

Figure 4.2 US Investment Performance Comparison 1926–1988

The great contribution that **Modern Portfolio Theory** made to investment theory and practice was to define a formal risk/return framework in which investment decisions could be undertaken in a scientific manner. By introducing a mathematical approach to asset selection and portfolio management, Markowitz moved investment thinking forward and added a more rigorous intellectual overlay.

By comparing the mean-variance footprint of different assets, **Modern Portfolio Theory** can be used to optimise a portfolio of assets to achieve an expected rate of return with the lowest possible dispersion risk. Since we can set an infinite number of possible performance levels, there must be an infinite number of corresponding portfolios. We can plot all these possible outcomes. When we do, they describe a curve as shown in Figure 4.3 below. The curve shows the best dispersion risk/return portfolios which can be devised from the assets available. At any point on the curve we can extract the exact composition of the corresponding portfolio. The example only shows two asset classes, emerging markets and major markets. Of course it could include many more if required.

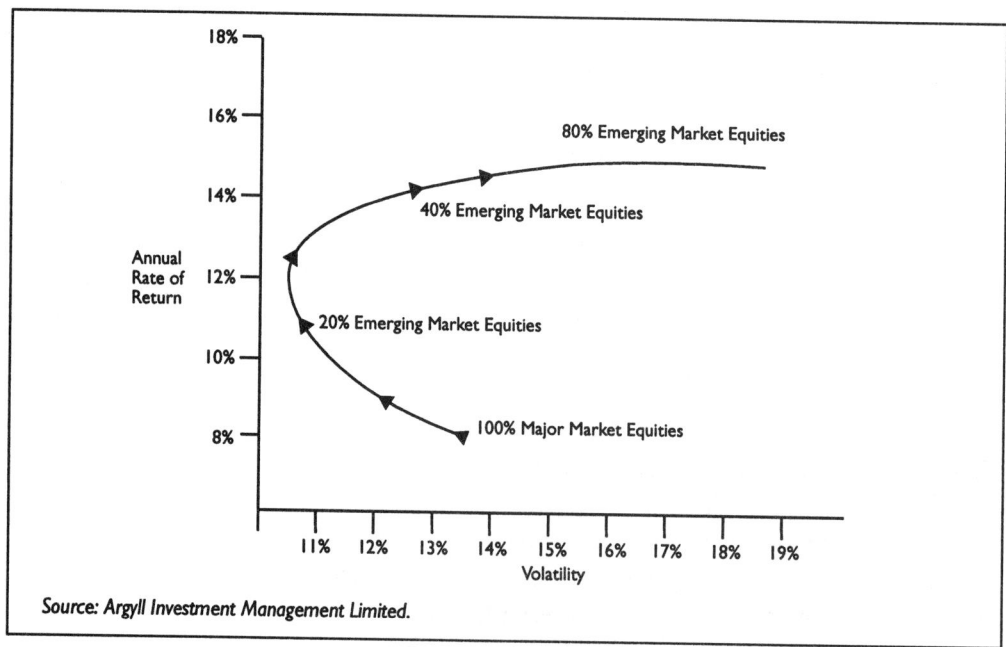

Source: Argyll Investment Management Limited.

Figure 4.3 The Efficient Frontier Curve for an optimised portfolio consisting of major market equities and emerging market equities.

Although mean-variance lies at the heart of **Modern Portfolio** optimisation theory it is also the reason why this theory is considered to be merely part of the wider **Post Modern Portfolio Theory**[6] which includes all distributions and not just normal ones. For this reason the original theory has limited practical uses since we know few distributions in the investment world are normal.

In addition the original notion that the standard deviation is a reasonable, all-embracing, measure of risk is no longer acceptable. Generally we consider that standard deviation is a statistical measure of variability: further that most investors prefer less volatile returns to more volatile returns. This simple idea, however, is not always quite so easy to accept in practice as we illustrate in the examples on page 100.

Consider the investments in Figures 4.4 and 4.5, labelled A and B. In the case of A, the investment return comes from a normal distribution with a mean of 10% and a standard deviation of 5% per annum. The other example, B, is a more volatile investment although it has the same mean return as A. Its standard deviation, however, is twice that of A ie. 10% per annum.

6. I am grateful to the *Journal of Investing* for letting me reproduce Figures 4.4–4.10 shown in the remainder of this chapter. These have been taken from the Fall, 1994 issue and specifically two articles, one by Dr. Leslie Balzer and the other by Brian Rom and Kathleen Ferguson.

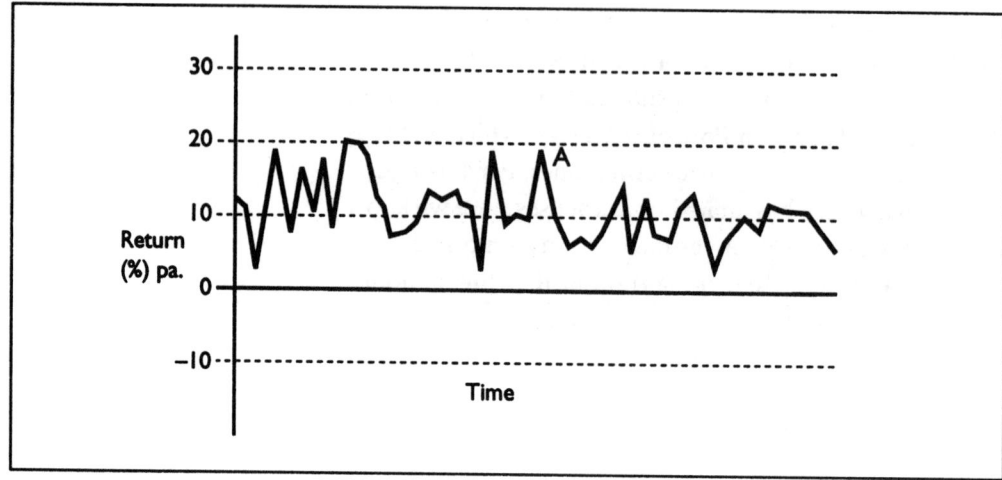

Figure 4.4 *Lower–Volatility Investment (A) Standard Deviation = 5% pa. Mean = 10% pa.*

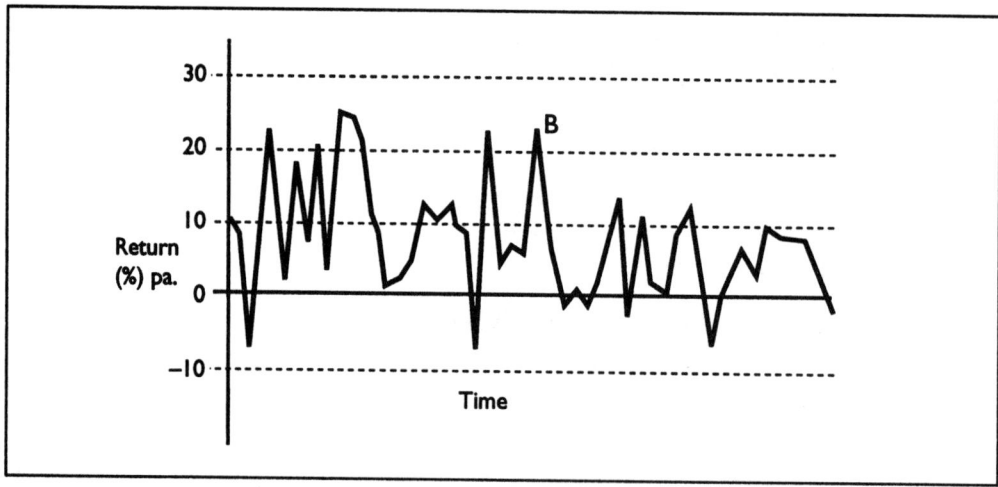

Figure 4.5 *Higher–Volatility Investment (B) Standard Deviation = 10% pa. Mean = 10% pa.*

Of course most people would feel that B is much more risky than A because it is more volatile.

If we overlay A over B then the situation becomes even clearer. See Figure 4.6 on page 101. Here the overlap clearly shows that the risk of B is greater than A.

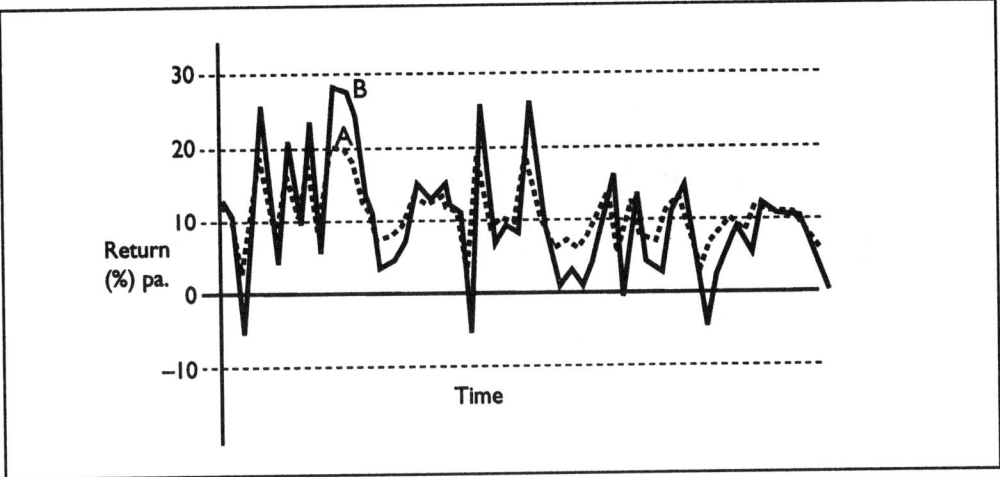

Figure 4.6 Higher and Lower-Volatility Investments with equal Means of A and B = 10% pa. Standard Deviation of A = 5% pa. and B = 10% pa.

If, however, we now introduce a new asset C as in Figure 4.7 on page 102, with a higher mean than B but the same standard deviation, we see an interesting development. The standard deviation of C is twice that of A, so according to **Modern Portfolio Theory** it is a riskier asset. Unfortunately, intuitively most investors would find C to be less risky than A, the exact opposite of what the theory suggests. If **Modern Portfolio Theory** is a good risk measure it should accord with intuition, which it does not always do.

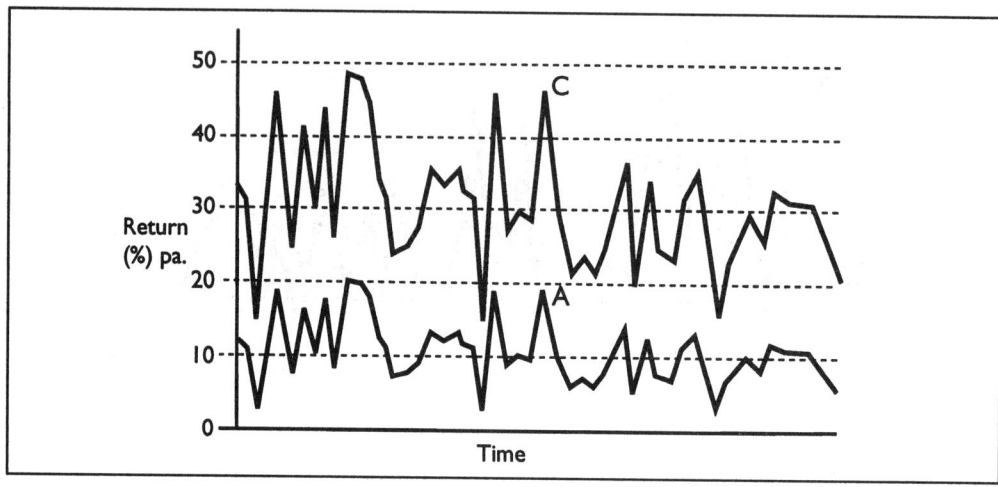

Figure 4.7 Higher and Lower–Volatility Investments with unequal Means.
Standard Deviations: A= 5% pa. and C = B = 10% pa.

In Figure 4.8 on page 103, D has the same standard deviation as B (and also C) but a lower average rate of return. Since their standard deviations are the same, **Modern Portfolio Theory** would suggest they have the same degree of riskiness. Most investors would disagree. Obviously D gives negative returns consistently, and would never be held as an asset, while C gives good positive returns and would always be the preferred asset.

The key points against using standard deviation as the single measurement of risk are therefore:

- intuitively reasonable results only occur when the means are equal or close to equal.

- the ranking of risk across portfolios is sometimes the opposite of intuitive rankings.

- equal numerical measurements of risk sometimes lead to large differences at the intuitive level.

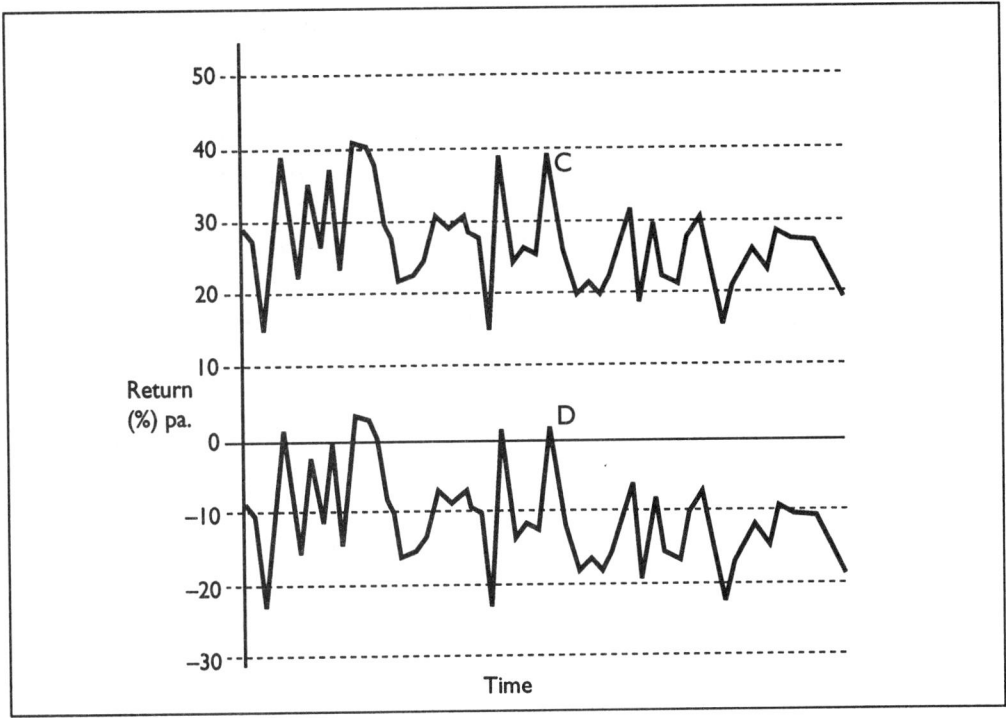

Figure 4.8 Equal–Volatility Investments with unequal Means. Standard Deviations: D=C=B=10% pa. Means: C=30% pa.; D= –10% pa.

Markowitz and the other great investment theorist of the day, William Sharpe, both realised that **Modern Portfolio Theory** was subject to important constraints and in certain situations the mean-variance methodology could lead to irrational predictions of behaviour. Markowitz noted early on that a model based on semi-variance would be preferable, but because computing was in its infancy, he lacked the number processing power to pursue this path. So he settled on using variance or standard deviation as his measure of risk.

But what is semi-variance? As we have seen,

calculations of the standard deviation of return begin with deviations from the mean return. Above-average returns lead to positive deviations, and below-average returns to negative deviations. Adding all the deviations together gives a meaningless zero result.

To get round this problem, the deviations are squared so they are all positive before adding them. The average of the squared deviations is then determined. Finally the square root is taken to return the dimension and units of measurement to those of the original time series. By squaring the numbers, the positive and negative deviations from the mean all contribute equally to the standard deviation.

This last stage is where the problem lies. Using standard deviation as a risk measurement results in above mean outperformance being penalised to the same extent as shortfalls below the mean. This is counter-intuitive and cannot be reconciled in the mind of the rational investor. From observations like this we must conclude that our intuitive feel for risk is not straightforward. It is somehow connected to a relative, not absolute concept of performance, which can be described as "the probability of under-performing some reference level." This seems reasonable, since investment managers tend to lose clients for failing to meet a performance objective rather than exceeding it.

POST MODERN PORTFOLIO THEORY

The great intellectual leap forward from **Modern Portfolio Theory** comes in the recognition that variance only measures the dispersion risks associated with achieving the average return. **Post Modern Portfolio**

Theory recognises that investment risk is only related to failing to achieve a minimum acceptable return, set by the investor. In essence, any return below the *Minimum Acceptable Return* is risk. Anything above is opportunity, and no investor should care how much opportunity he is exposed to. We have attempted to show this idea visually below in Figure 4.9.

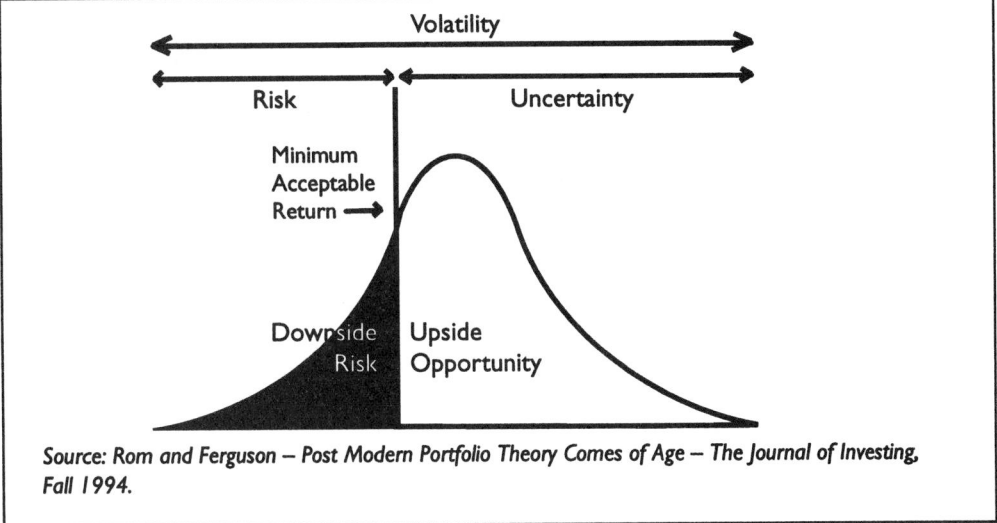

Source: Rom and Ferguson – Post Modern Portfolio Theory Comes of Age – The Journal of Investing, Fall 1994.

Figure 4.9 Downside Risk and Upside Opportunity

In the above Figure, downside risk is represented by the area shown in black. This risk can be split into two components, each of which can be separately analysed. These two elements are known as downside probability and average downside magnitude. Downside probability simply measures the probability of underperforming the *Minimum Acceptable Return,* while the average downside magnitude measures the average shortfall below the *Minimum Acceptable Return* when it is not reached. We thus have the ability to measure how likely it is that we shall underperform the *Minimum Acceptable Return,* and how much this underperformance will be on average. These parameters far better define risk than the more simplistic standard deviation.

When using **Modern Portfolio Theory** and **Post Modern Portfolio Theory** to run optimisation programmes, a statistical return distribution must be specified for each asset type. Again **Modern Portfolio Theory** is limited since it can only cope with the two parameter normal distribution (ie. mean/variance). In contrast, **Post Modern Portfolio Theory** is much more versatile and can use a wide range of asymmetrical (skewed) as well as symmetrical distributions. How much of a problem is skewedness? In the example below, Figure 4.10, we show a number of examples from real life:

PERIOD ENDING 31.12.92	10 Years	20 Years	30 Years
ASSET			
Large-Cap Stocks	1.80	1.23	0.89
Small-Cap Stocks	1.07	1.22	1.14
Foreign Stocks	0.92	1.10	n/a
Bonds	0.83	0.94	0.97
Cash	0.64	1.25	1.11
Inflation	0.82	1.35	3.03

Source: Rom and Ferguson – Post Modern Portfolio Theory Comes of Age – The Journal of Investing, Fall 1994.

Figure 4.10 Skewedness of Major Asset Classes and Inflation.

Any significant divergence from 1.0 indicates a high level of skewedness. The table clearly shows there is considerable skewedness across all the asset classes which cannot be described by the simple mean/variance model. **Modern Portfolio Theory,** therefore, is not powerful enough to deal adequately with real investment data. We therefore need the more powerful **Post Modern Portfolio Theory** to deal with real life skewed investment data.

Finally, we should not underestimate the usefulness of the *Minimum Acceptable Return* concept. For individuals, this may be the building society deposit rate; for a pension fund's trustees, the actuarial rate of return; and for the investment manager of the pension fund's assets, the industry's median investment return. There is an infinite number of potential *Minimum Acceptable Returns* and, for each, there is an optimum portfolio which reaches this goal with the lowest expected risk using a mix of the available assets. Plotting all these potential *Minimum Acceptable Return* portfolios creates a curve called the efficient frontier similar to the one we saw in Figure 4.3 on page 98. At any point on this curve we can find the composition of the optimum portfolio which corresponds to these risk/return characteristics. This opens the window to a whole new host of risk/return modelling possibilities.

CONCLUSION

There has been a great deal written about risk by the theorists and by investors. **Modern Portfolio Theory** handles all uncertainty in the same manner, penalising upside gains as heavily as downside losses, and portraying uncertainty as a symmetrical risk measure. This is not a realistic reflection of life and the behaviour of investors. They may imagine their sole objective is to make money. It is not. In reality, they are deeply concerned with downside risk because of personal financial commitments to the family and home. This is why so many people follow the sensible policy of keeping a proportion of their capital in National Savings or building societies. Risk is not symmetrical in the eyes of the investor, but heavily skewed by fear towards the downside.

The acceleration in research into this subject has in part been due to the expansion in the use of more esoteric financial instruments which offer asymmetrical payoffs and therefore cannot be adequately analysed using conventional measures of risk ie. variance or standard deviation. Hence risk measurement now concentrates on the downside tail of the distribution curve, below the benchmark performance target, a variable set as a preference by each investor.

As we have seen, the shortcomings of **Modern Portfolio Theory** are the assumptions that the variance of portfolio returns is the right risk measurement and that investment returns from all assets and individual investments follow a normal distribution pattern. Neither assumption is correct. Although earlier we referred to standard deviation as the measure of risk, it is now evident that it is not specific enough to be given this label. What we can say is that standard deviation is a measure of uncertainty, and it is easy to see the intuitive jump to say uncertainty must equal risk. Risk, however, is not necessarily the same as uncertainty. Generally risk is uncertainty which may lead to an unpleasant outcome, while opportunity is uncertainty which leads to a pleasant outcome.

Recently with the advent of more powerful computers and major advances in modern financial theories, we have been able to overcome the initial constraints of **Modern Portfolio Theory.** We now view **Post Modern Portfolio Theory** as the general theory of which **Modern Portfolio Theory** is a special case covering symmetrical only distributions.

Hedge funds, through the skill of their managers, try to reduce downside risk, so their return characteristics will certainly not conform to a normal distribution curve. If they are successful, their distribution curve will be quite positively skewed and will display a small tail below the *Minimum Acceptable Return*. Because of this, **Modern Portfolio Theory** optimisation programmes, which cannot deal adequately with skewed distributions, undervalue their contribution to a portfolio which also contains conventional assets. Only **Post Modern Portfolio Theory** techniques can make the necessary allowances to show the full benefits of including these funds in portfolios. The results lead to a heavy weighting in hedge funds compared to conventional long-only investments, because of their enhanced risk/return characteristics.

HEDGE FUNDS VERSUS OTHER INVESTMENTS

Investing is as much a philosophical as a financial challenge. At its most basic it involves channelling one resource into another to produce greater value. The resource could be time invested into learning to gain knowledge and understanding, or money invested in the stockmarket to create wealth. If for simplicity we restrict ourselves solely to financial investments, we are talking about buying something today which will be worth more later; or selling something we do not have, but which we have borrowed, in the hope of buying it back in the future for less than we sold it for.

In theory, the range of possible investments is enormous, but for practical purposes the list is much reduced. For example, who knows much about Picasso? How many people would be competent to give advice on buying one of his paintings? If you bought a Picasso, even at the right price, how easy would it be to sell? Where would you keep it and who could you tell? Tempting though it might be to dream, actually buying a Picasso would be a nightmare for most people. And as an investment for the professional, it is impossible to sell short. Investing in real property has a similar list of drawbacks. Property has to be insured. If it is to retain its value, it needs maintenance. And tenants must be found to produce income from it.

Sadly, works of art and property must be crossed off any list of potential investments, taking us back to bonds, equities, commodity and financial futures or investment funds containing these instruments. We know where we are with them. They have limited custodial problems, we can price them easily, deal in them easily, and receive proceeds from their sale rapidly. For these reasons, it is worth considering only these types of investments as alternatives to hedge funds.

THE COMPARISON

Bonds are conventionally considered a low-risk investment compared to equities and hedge funds and in the short term, this is normally so. As a result their expected long-term return will be below that of equities. If this were not so, then businesses would cease to expand using share capital. Instead they would repay debts and buy bonds in preference to expanding their operations. From time to time, when real interest rates are very high, this does happen for short periods. But this is not a sustainable position for an economy seeking to generate increasing wealth and an increasing standard of living.

In 1994 bonds proved to be far more volatile than equities, but this was unusual. It was due to a number of "long only" US leveraged funds being forced to cut their positions as US interest rates rose and losses mounted.

This selling created a domino effect. As stock was dumped on the market, prices plummeted. The equity market escaped serious harm because the same one way bet had not been taken on equities.

Viewed from a non-traditional perspective, bonds can be shown to be extremely high-risk long-term investments. For example, someone buying gilts in 1936 as a safe long-term investment, according to the January 1996 BZW Equity-Gilt Study, would still be showing no real gain 60 years later at the end of 1995. In contrast, a UK equity portfolio performing in line with the market would have risen by an annualised real 5.9% pa. Taking a more recent example, since 1970 gilts have achieved a real return of 3.1% pa. compared to 7.3% pa. on equities. In both cases a positive result, but again equities are well ahead.

Over the long term equities have been a much better investment than bonds if capital gains and income are combined. Equities have generally been more volatile and therefore traditionally considered more risky than bonds. Using the **Post Modern Portfolio Theory** definition of risk the positions are reversed. As real gilt returns have been so low and poor in comparison to equities they have continually failed to reach a realistic minimum acceptable return. Bonds consequently have been expensive to hold in performance terms and should be classified as high risk. Later we shall see how hedge funds compare to equities.

Leaving aside the "real" long-term rates of return, over shorter periods all of the classes of investments we are considering have one thing in common – if you get your timing wrong when you purchase them it can take a long while before you recover your initial stake money, even in nominal terms. Dealing in options and futures, you may never get your stake money back. In general, however, even if you invest in UK equities at the peak of a market cycle, you can expect to be back in profit within five years.

With hedge funds investment timing is less relevant. For those funds at the speculative end of the spectrum there is no way of assessing whether you should be buying or selling on past experience. At the other extreme, surprisingly, the low risk funds are also largely insensitive to cycles – stockmarket or others. The skilful manager is just as likely to do well when stockmarkets are rising as when they are falling. Indeed, part of the attraction of hedge funds is that in most cases their performance is un-correlated to that of other investments or markets. The exception is the group of funds in the middle of the risk range which pursue strategies related to stock futures, markets or specific sectors within them. Here there is some positive correlation. Otherwise investment timing is irrelevant and there is no evidence that it can improve performance when buying hedge funds. This should be a truism since one of the aims and benefits of hedge funds is to remove market risk.

Many investors find the volatility of stockmarkets uncomfortable. They are constantly torn between the two great emotions of fear and greed. When markets are rising, greed is at work; "Why aren't I fully invested? Look at the opportunity I am missing." In falling markets, the boot is on the other foot; "Why am I fully invested and losing money?" We all know how easy it is to let these emotions gain the upper hand over rational analysis, and to find ourselves buying near the top, selling near the bottom. Only after years of experience do we finally learn that market timing is dreadfully difficult and it is usually far better for a long-only investor always to be exposed to the market. Since the markets tend to rise over the long term, being uninvested at any point is a dangerous strategy.

Of course some disagree and suggest market timing can add value. They claim that unit trust advisers, in particular, are driven by self interest to advise their clients to sit still and stay fully invested, come what may. They do not agree with the notion that it is not timing that matters, but time itself, and short-term volatility is part and parcel of long-term investing. They claim that the advisers are largely driven by not wanting to see large flows of money forever wandering in and out of client portfolios. Further, that the "buy and hold" strategy benefits the adviser because of the "trailer" fees received. These are payments made by some unit trusts to advisers and paid out of the annual management fee for as long as the client remains in that fund. They provide a higher quality of earnings to advisers than fees earned by dealing on the client's portfolio. Instead of the usual criticism of churning the adviser is in danger of being accused of under managing clients' portfolios. In reality, experience suggests that low turnover generally benefits rather than hampers the performance of any portfolio.

The evidence available, however, does not completely support the fully invested, low turnover view. In 1993, a study of the US market by the University of Michigan suggested that if an investor had been liquid during the market's top 20 days over the five years before the 1987 Crash, he would have cut his overall return in half. On the other hand the same study suggests that between 1963 and 1993, missing the market's worst 90 days would have also increased annual returns. Using the S&P 500 as a benchmark, the in/out investor would have generated an annual return of 21.7%, against 11.8% on a buy and hold strategy.

Interestingly, if you had missed the best and worst 90 days, you would have still benefited overall. So is there more benefit in dodging the bad days than danger in missing the good? In reality, no-one gets the market right on a daily basis, and the costs of dealing would count against a heavy in/out strategy. Successfully trading the stockmarket requires two correct decisions every time – buying and selling. Since most professional investors would be pleased to get 7 out of 10 decisions correct, to be consistently right trading daily is a skill few possess. So the case in favour of buy and hold strategies improves significantly.

PERFORMANCE – RISK/RETURN

Perhaps more than anything else, investors are concerned with "performance". This can be looked upon as a combination of risk and return. Primarily investors are interested in future performance. They need to know how their own or potential investments have performed in the past in order to improve their performance in the future. But performance cannot be measured purely on an absolute scale, since some assets are more likely to produce a greater overall return than others and for different levels of risk.

As we have seen already there is a very strong relationship between risk and return. For instance, betting on a single spin of a coin where each participant puts the same amount into the pot is high risk. You win or lose immediately. If the rules are winner takes all, you either double your money or lose the lot. To most people this would be recognised for what it is, blind speculation. If, however, the game is decided over 100 throws and each player has sufficient resources to cover a bad run, the character of the game changes. It becomes one of low risk and low return for each player, since each is likely to win 50% of the time over such a large number of throws, and therefore each will end up with their original money more or less intact. If one player does not have the resources to cover a bad run, the risk profile changes, depending on how much resource he does have. If, for instance, he can only suffer two losses in a row, he is likely to be wiped out within eight throws. If he can sustain ten losses in a row, then on average he should survive 150 throws.

If we alter the odds by saying that we will play the game 100 times, and that player A will only put half the stake of player B into the pot on each play, the characteristics of the game change significantly. Player A is now in an enviable position. If we assume each player can suffer 15 losses in a row, although we still only expect A to win 50% of the time, each time he wins, he wins twice his stake while B when he wins only wins half his stake. Assuming the coin falls fairly then after 100 throws we would reasonably expect A to have won about 50 times, winning 100 (50 x 2) times his stake and on the 50 losing occasions he loses 50 (50 x 1) his stake. He therefore finishes a net 50 times up on his initial stake of 1.

This example shows that it is not only important how many times we win, but also how much we win relative to our stake money. That determines our overall level of return. We can win a little often for a low-risk, low-return investment. Or we can go for the big one. Most players/investors prefer to aim for a more middle course and spread their capital over a number of different games/investments to produce a balanced portfolio of risk and return.

Measuring absolute return in isolation for long-only portfolios is not particularly relevant, since we do not know what risks were taken to achieve that return. So investors look for benchmarks or standards against which they can compare their performance. An investor may buy one share and compare its performance against the FT-SE Actuaries All-Share Index. This is not really comparing like with like, since the index is comprised of hundreds of shares which in aggregate are heavily diversified. If our share happens to be an oil exploration company, it could produce fantastic returns, or it could go bust. In all probability, the index cannot go to zero. So this is a poor comparison.

On the other hand, a diversified portfolio of shares can reasonably be compared to the index and this produces meaningful results. If, for example, the portfolio displays the same beta as the market – that is, it has the same risk characteristics – but has a higher annualised return, then for the same level of risk as the market we are getting a higher rate of return. This is a good portfolio. These same rules hold true for bonds and bond portfolios, whether held directly or through a unit trust or an investment trust.

Hedge funds are different and comparison is more difficult. Hedge funds are primarily not interested in relative performance, only absolute returns. Comparing a traditional portfolio against an index is fine in principle, but what happens if the market slumps? Even if our portfolio has outperformed, we have still lost a large part of our investment. Hedge funds aim to produce positive results at all times, and are not concerned in matching an index step for step. Their rationale is two-fold. You do not win prizes for losing money, even if you have beaten the index. And if you are going to take additional risks, the potential payoffs must justify them. We cannot therefore satisfactorily compare hedge funds against an index. We can, however, construct a risk and return matrix and see how hedge fund returns measure up against the level of risk required to achieve them. We can then gauge the relative performance of each fund by examining the ratio of investment return to the amount of risk taken. This will allow us to compare different investment styles on a level playing field

This is the basis of the Sharpe Ratio which can roughly be described as the measure of return per unit of risk. Using the Sharpe Ratio can produce interesting results. If investors A and B begin the year with equal capital, even if A, at the end of the year, is up on B he cannot necessarily be considered the better investor. If A has incurred very large volatility of returns on a monthly basis, while B has produced very steady returns, then B may be the better investor. For instance, take the following figures:

Risk free rate of return in the period (US T-bills) = 5%

A's return in the period – 50%   A's standard deviation of returns – 25%

B's return in the period – 35%   B's standard deviation of returns – 15%

$$\text{Sharpe Ratio} = \frac{\text{Annualised RoR of Portfolio} - \text{Risk free RoR}}{\text{Standard Deviation of Returns}}$$

$$\text{Sharpe Ratio of A} = \frac{50 - 5}{25} = 1.8$$

$$\text{Sharpe Ratio of B} = \frac{35 - 5}{15} = 2.0$$

According to Sharpe, B is actually a better investor than A because he has taken far less risk to reach his returns.

Figure 5.1 below shows the risk and return characteristics of major asset types compared to various hedge fund strategies, over the five year period to 31.12.95. For an indicative measure of risk we are using the Sharpe Ratio, the higher this figure the better.

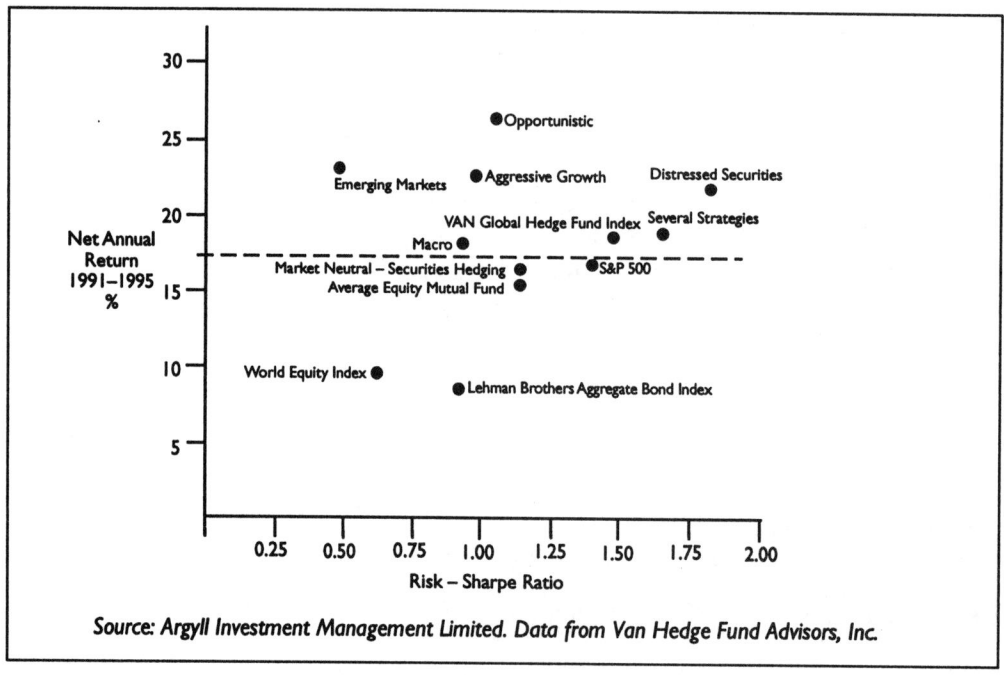

Figure 5.1 Risk and return results for major asset types and various hedge fund strategies over the five year period to 31.12.95.

It is fascinating to note the superior figures for most of the hedge products compared to more conventional investments. The Distressed Securities hedge fund strategy has the highest Sharpe Ratio, slightly better than the Several Strategies and the VAN Global Hedge Fund Index.

In general hedge products have high returns for a given Sharpe Ratio. This should not be surprising from what we have said about the innate advantages these funds have in their ability to reduce risk by gearing up and simultaneously going short. What is surprising is that these figures have not attracted more attention. Look at the position of the Average Equity Mutual Fund. It has a similar return but a lower Sharpe Ratio than the S&P 500; but it comes nowhere near hedge funds in performance terms. These generally have higher performance and higher Sharpe Ratios. While the case in favour of hedge funds, however, is very strong, it is not proven. Nevertheless, why don't more people switch to these types of investments in the US? The answer is relatively straightforward and lies in the next two sections – *Structure* and *Marketing*.

STRUCTURE

Not only do hedge funds have different and usually less well understood investment styles compared to most mutual funds, but they also have a different legal structure. Historically in the US most hedge funds were structured as limited partnerships. These are limited to 99 or fewer (qualified) investors by the Investment Company Act of 1940. The advantage of the Limited Partnership is that the fund does not have to list with the SEC, and therefore bypasses onerous reporting requirements. At the same time, in order to make the funds viable, each investor had to put up a relatively large amount of money, anywhere from US$100,000 to US$5million. Anything much smaller, say US$5,000, would result in too small a fund to be viable. Hedge funds tended to become the exclusive preserve of the very wealthy, and the ordinary man in the street has not been able to access them. This is why mutual funds, despite their poorer relative performance, have not suffered at the hands of hedge funds to the extent one might have imagined.

The concept of an investment partnership is largely restricted to the US and there are a number of entities involved:

General Partner – this is normally an individual, limited partnership or a limited liability company. The capital introduced into the fund from this source is essentially the fund manager's own direct interest in the fund. Often the partnership agreement will stipulate the minimum interest that the general partner must maintain in the fund at all times. This gives some comfort to the limited partners that the manager is risking his or her capital as well.

The general partner does, however, benefit in other ways for his services as the manager of the partnership. There is usually an incentive fee on the capital appreciation of the fund, giving the general partner anywhere from 15% to 50% of the gross profits of the fund. The usual figure seems to come out around 25%. This reward is not straightforward. Often conditions are set. The most common is the "high-water mark". This means that the general partner can only start to benefit when the loss from any previous downturn has been recovered, and the Net Asset Value of the fund reaches a new high.

Limited Partner – these are the investors in the fund, limited to 99 in total. If there were more, the fund would automatically be regulated by the SEC. In addition under the Employment Retirement Income Security Act of 1974 (ERISA) not more than 25% of the fund's assets can be held by pension funds.

Management Company – this is the entity which manages the fund's administration and accounting. The company is almost always owned by the same people who own the General Partnership, and receives its remuneration through an annual fee based on the net assets of the fund, usually around 0.75% to 2%.

Prime Broker – owing to the complexity of some hedge funds arising from the range of instruments they use, funds have found it easier to deal with one head broker. In addition, since the basis of hedge fund management is in balancing long and short positions, this can only be achieved with the help of a central processing facility. If this were not available, hedge funds could not easily finance their long positions from their short ones. The prime broker, normally a major broking house, under-takes the coordination of all trades, including taking care of settlement and the custody of securities. It does not necessarily execute all trades, since these are often carried out by execution-only brokers who report back to the prime broker and to the hedge fund manager with details of trades, but look to the prime broker for settlement.

Although historically most US based hedge funds have been set up as limited partnerships, this is changing. Most states have now passed legislation allowing limited liability companies to be used as the hedge fund's legal vehicle. Assuming the managers form the company in the correct manner, the tax consequences to the investor are very similar to those of a limited partnership.

MARKETING

Hedge Funds – offering participation in a private investment partnership or fund requires the partnership to
create a private placement under the Securities Act 1933,
as amended. Further if the fund intends to invest in
commodities, it must comply with the disclosure
requirements of the Commodity Exchange Act (CEA).
There are other lesser legal requirements but these are
beyond the scope of this book. The fund must show that
each investor has complied with these disclosures and
must therefore receive from each investor a completed
subscription document containing all relevant information
and disclosures. This can be quite an onerous document
to complete.

Since these funds are established by private placing,
they are by definition fairly discreet vehicles. Under SEC
regulations their use of advertising is very strictly
controlled. It is not surprising that many of the best
funds are still relatively unknown to advisers and the
public, but this is changing. In order to attract more
clients and funds under management, many limited
partnerships have set up satellite offshore funds. Indeed
most non-US hedge funds are now formed as offshore
investment vehicles. The funds are usually based in a
jurisdiction where there is minimal taxation, such as the
British Virgin Islands, the Cayman Islands, Bermuda, the
Isle of Man, Netherlands Antilles and more recently
Dublin. In these centres the administration of the funds
is undertaken, although custody is often managed
elsewhere and in a different jurisdiction. The investment
adviser may be based in a major financial centre but not
necessarily so and will possess delegated powers from

the fund's offshore management company to trade on the fund's behalf in investments. Though these new offshore funds lie outside US jurisdiction, a number still require rigorous questionnaires to be completed before a purchase can be made.

Unit Trusts – in contrast to hedge funds, the structure of UK unit trusts is much more straightforward. The aims of unit trusts are similar to those of hedge funds. They allow private investors to pool their monies into a vehicle which is professionally managed on their behalf. Investment decisions are made on behalf of the unit trust holders, stock is held in safe custody by a neutral entity, investment records are kept by the administrator and a report is made twice a year to each member outlining the progress of the fund. The fund is audited annually, as are hedge funds, and the affairs of the members are well protected.

A unit trust which is marketed to the public needed in the past to be authorised by the Department of Trade and Industry, though responsibility for authorisation has passed to the Securities and Investments Board. There are also unauthorised trusts which some stockbrokers, for example, manage for their clients. Unauthorised property unit trusts are permitted to offer to pension funds a form of collective investment in property. Advertisements for unit trusts are closely monitored and must contain a health warning – a reminder that the unit price can go down as well as up. Unauthorised unit trusts have even tighter marketing restrictions than authorised unit trusts.

When they are first launched, unit trusts make a fixed price offer for a limited period – you will see the advertisements in the financial pages of the national papers, usually on a Saturday or Sunday. At this time

you can apply for units at a known price. The rest of the
time you pay the price ruling when your application is
received. Fund management groups also frequently
provide regular savings plans which allow you to pay so
much a month. The money is invested in units when it is
received.

Unit trusts must pay out the income they receive
on their investments to their unitholders, pro rata with
their holdings. Sometimes the investor has a choice
between income units (which receive a share of the
dividends in cash) and accumulation units (where a
share of the income is added to the value of each unit).
This second option is convenient, but does not offer any
tax saving: the income is reinvested net of basic rate tax
and any higher rate tax due has to be paid. However,
accumulation units are not charged with the cost of
reinvestment, and the investor also has a better record of
his total return when he keeps the same number of units.
An alternative is for the investor to be credited with
additional units representing the reinvested net income.
This may involve paying preliminary charges on the new
units.

The offshore and overseas funds are close relatives
of the unit trusts. They are not authorised unit trusts,
though they operate on the unit trust principle and many
operate under the umbrella of one of the fund management
groups that offers authorised unit trusts in the UK. Many
offshore funds are technically located in the Channel
Islands and managed from there, with the UK parent group
described as the "adviser" to the fund. Other popular
locations are Luxembourg and Dublin.

DEALING

As outlined above, you must complete a time-consuming questionnaire to buy hedge funds through a limited partnership or an offshore fund. Free funds must also be wired to the fund's administrator ahead of a purchase, so they arrive before or on the specified dealing day. Selling requires the completion of a redemption form which must be faxed to the administrator together with bank details for the remittance of funds. Having made an investment there is sometimes a lock-in period of up to one year during which time your shares cannot be sold. In addition, with or without a lock in, sometimes up to 90 days' notice must be given before a sale can be executed. Dealing terms and conditions vary widely. Finally, often there is a delay of anywhere from one week and in exceptional cases three months before proceeds are received although on average it takes nearer to two weeks after the dealing date.

Irrespective of if you are buying or selling hedge funds invariably only one price is quoted. This represents the net asset value per share of the fund.

There is also another important factor for the limited partner to consider. At the end of each period when the fund is available to receive subscriptions or satisfy redemptions, the assets must be valued. Accurate valuations are not always possible. While most securities, particularly listed ones, have readily available prices, the complex derivative trades undertaken by hedge funds often cannot be valued at market value, but only via some form of computer modelling programme. The real profit or loss of such trades can only be booked when they mature. That may not be for some time. To keep a fair balance of profit and loss among the partners, the funds which have a high percentage of their assets in such trades have devised a system of using what is known as the side pocket.

In its simplest form when the fund buys an illiquid investment it sets up a new account specifically for this trade and allocates each partner a pro rata share. New partners entering after this trade take no interest in it. Partners redeeming before the trade is closed out receive their capital back plus or minus losses, but have to wait for the side pocket trade to be closed before they get this part of their capital back, again plus or minus losses.

Offshore hedge funds generally do not use side pockets, but use equalisation accounts. In the case of a limited partnership, an incentive fee can be charged directly to each partner. This is not so easy for offshore funds with hundreds of shareholders. Equalisation allows investors coming into a fund during the course of the year not to be unfairly treated when the incentive fee is calculated. In this case often, when shareholders purchase shares, they have part of their subscription allocated to the equalisation account. At the end of the year, when the incentive fee is finally determined, a portion of the equalisation account is used to settle it. Anything left over is used to purchase more shares of the fund for the shareholder.

Unit trusts are much easier to deal in than hedge funds. You can often buy over the telephone, sending a cheque later in settlement. Some groups require a letter, however, and cheques to be cashed before processing any transactions, although this is usually only for direct dealings by private clients. You can usually sell by telephone sending the certificate, where there is one, on later. Proceeds are normally dispatched within seven days of the bargain date assuming the certificate has been received.

The drawback with unit trusts is their charging structure. There are two charges, a purchase or initial charge of around 5.25% of the value of the initial investment, which may in cases of larger transactions be reduced to nearer 0.5%, and an on-going annual charge of 1%–1.5% on the net asset value of the investment. Initial and annual charges have risen over the years, especially the annual rate. There is now pressure to reduce the front end charges. This is coming from the US, where no-load funds (no front end charges) are common. Indeed, some unit trusts are now structured with no initial charge, but with an "exit" charge diminishing over a period of years.

As with shares, there is not a single dealing price for the units. There is a buying price and a selling price: you buy the units from the managers at the higher "offer" price and receive the lower "bid" price when you sell them back. The price spread partially reflects the fact that the trust itself has to pay a higher price when it buys shares, and gets a lower price when it sells, and will incur dealing expenses. But the spread also includes the initial charge made by the managers and various other costs. If a unit trust suffers a large outflow of funds it has some leeway to move the bid and offer prices down to a lower level, known as a bid basis or liquidation basis.

Performance figures for unit trusts should always allow for the pricing spread. So if the quotation for a particular trust has moved up from 100p–107p to 120p–128p over the year, the calculation should allow for the fact that the investor would have bought at 107p and sold at 120p: a gain of 13p or 12.1%, not 21p or 19.6%. This is known as "offer to bid" performance.

SECURITY AND TAXATION

Since the limited partnership hedge funds in the US are not regulated by the SEC, they are potentially more open to abuse than regulated mutual funds. You should keep this in mind when considering a purchase. It is fair to say the incidence of abuse is very low. Perhaps the greatest abuse may be one of conflict of interest where a manager may also trade for his own or family accounts. He may potentially be in a position to benefit from passing the best deals through these accounts rather than to the partnership. Actual fraud or abscondment with monies is not something which has been recorded. There have on the other hand been cases of funds "blowing up", losing the capital of the fund, usually through excessive gearing in falling markets.

The securities themselves are invariably held by a safe custodian – either a major broking firm or a bank – and there is very limited risk of loss from this source. Mis-pricing could occur and has occurred where the deeds of the partnership have allowed the managing partner to value shares or trades at his own value rather than the market valuation. This happens in exceptional conditions, usually where the manager feels the market price is way out of line with the correct price owing to abnormal market conditions.

Offshore hedge funds are potentially prone to similar shortcomings since, in most jurisdictions where they operate, the regulatory authorities are largely absent or have weak powers. Taxation issues are more complex. The onshore US limited partnership funds follow the conduit principle of taxation. Under this, a partnership's income, expenses, gains and losses flow through to its partners and are taxed at the partner level rather than higher up. This removes problems of double taxation, and simplifies the tax returns of the individual partners.

Offshore hedge funds are generally not subject to taxation, apart from any taxes levied on individual holdings, such as withholding taxes. Shareholders do not have any taxation worries. Since these funds tend to accumulate income and do not make distributions, all gains are of a capital nature. Of course, anyone resident for taxation purposes within the UK would be obliged to report any realised gains to the Inland Revenue.

UK unit trusts, authorised or unauthorised, come under a special group of rules within the UK tax system, similar to the US conduit principle. They do not pay capital gains taxes, but advance corporation tax is paid on dividends distributed by the funds. This can be reclaimed for non tax payers. The offshore funds operate under the tax regime of the country where they are located. This is usually more beneficial than that of Great Britain. For a British investor resident in the UK, there is no tax advantage in using them. As far as the Inland Revenue is concerned, these investments are treated as if they were normal unit trusts.

For expatriates, the picture can be a little different. Those working in low taxation areas such as the Middle East, and paying little or no UK tax, gain some benefits with offshore funds compared to UK unauthorised unit trusts. For low or zero yielding growth trusts which invest in areas where the yield on the underlying shares is very low, the advantages are modest. The other major difference from the unit trust is that offshore funds are usually denominated in US$.

MONITORING PERFORMANCE

Performance statistics for unit trusts and offshore funds are readily available and closely followed by the investing community. For the institutional investor Micropal is the best known and most advanced measurement system. It is available in hard copy and computer form. The computer data is easily manipulated and can be helpful in comparing funds from different areas. The latest Windows software makes it easy to import data and charts straight into reports for a very professional presentation.

The most widely read source of statistics is probably the monthly magazine *Money Management*, which provides a fairly complete list of funds showing how £1,000 invested over various time periods would have grown. As with any range of investments, performance varies widely within sectors and from sector to sector.

The performance of offshore funds is available in a number of publications, the most notable being *Offshore Investor* and *Expat*. The figures tend to be presented in terms of percentage return over various periods, usually 1, 3, 6 months and 1, 2, 3, 5 years. Interestingly these publications also cover futures funds and hedge funds, but only in a limited way.

Data on hedge funds is surprisingly sparse in the UK. Funds are not always eager to publish their performance or even publicise their existence. The position is improving as we show in Chapter 6 and in the UK we do now have dedicated providers of information. The cost of this information is, however, much higher than that for unit and investment trusts. This reflects the difficulty in obtaining it.

Summary

Hedge funds and traditional UK pooled investment funds do differ in:

- Performance characteristics
- Structure
- Marketing
- Dealing
- Taxation

The differences are not as great as you might think in practice and after the first few deals transactions become quite straightforward. Hedge funds are probably not as well regulated as other funds nor are they as secure. On the other hand their overall performance tends to be better. Careful selection will help avoid many of the pitfalls and we will tackle this point in more depth in Chapter 6.

* * *

6

HOW TO ACCESS AND ASSESS HEDGE FUNDS

Until recently, it was difficult to get information on hedge funds in this country. The picture is starting to change. At least once a week, the financial press carries an article on them. More and more people are reading about hedge funds regularly, although most investors still find it hard to come by detailed information on individual funds. Perhaps because of this, most UK investors have been reluctant to venture into hedge funds. Active investment has been confined largely to a few specialist investment managers, generally those looking after wealthy international clients. The rest have stood on the side lines, marvelling at how the likes of George Soros and his Quantum Fund have achieved such amazing returns. The lack of any great surge of demand for these eye-catching vehicles is probably due to basic supply-side economics. There is a strong latent need for these funds, but because they have not been made readily available to investors, no demand has been developed. If the funds will not come to the investors, how do the investors go to the funds?

PICKING THE RIGHT VEHICLE

Before covering information sources and the means of access to hedge fund managers, it is important to consider which of the various investment structures available is most suited to a UK investor's needs.

In order to back the manager they prefer, investors can buy straight into an existing investment vehicle. This will usually be a limited partnership for onshore US investors, or a company for offshore funds. Alternatively, the really wealthy can consider setting up a managed account, which is essentially a personal portfolio. There are pros and cons for both routes, but generally only very wealthy individuals or institutions can really opt for the managed account.

Investment via an existing fund is relatively straightforward. Although most will only accept an initial minimum sum, this is usually way below the published figure, which is often around US$1million. Other benefits from buying into an existing fund are limited liability, zero or low set-up costs, and prices which can often be found in the *International Herald Tribune* or the *Financial Times*. There are drawbacks. Liquidity is limited, and it may be possible only to withdraw money monthly, or even quarterly. In some cases, funds may not be released until two months after a sale. Investors may also have to settle for out-of-date and partial information on what the fund is invested in, and have no control over the structure and terms of the fund, covering matters like brokerage fees and other arrangements.

By contrast, a managed account provides far more information on what investment positions are being taken. Provided the agreement has been drawn up in a sensible fashion, liquidity is considerably better, and daily reports on performance are often available. There are some disadvantages, including heavy costs of setting up, the lack of limited liability and, of course, the need for a much larger minimum investment. Figure 6.1 below gives a comparison between the various options.

TYPE OF PRODUCT	POSITIVES	NEGATIVES
Limited Partnership	No or low set up charges	Variable liquidity Large minimum investment
Offshore Fund	Deals at NAV Lower minimum investment Limited liability	No control over structure or terms Tardy and often poor reporting
Managed Account	Knowledge of exact positions held Individual negotiation of terms Personal service High liquidity	High organisation costs High minimum investment No limited liability

Figure 6.1 A Comparison of Hedge Fund Vehicles

For UK investors, private or institutional, the most sensible and certainly the easiest route is through an offshore fund, as explained in the rest of this chapter.

As we have shown in Chapter 5, administratively there are many similarities between offshore hedge funds and unit trusts. The main differences are that offshore hedge funds usually trade at Net Asset Value, and do not bear a front end load. A growing number of UK unit trusts are copying the US move towards a no-load, single price structure, but most are still quoted with a bid/offer spread. Hedge funds generally only trade once a month, while unit trusts generally set prices and trade daily. There are differences between unit trusts and offshore hedge funds, but they are not enormous.

FINDING OUT ABOUT FUNDS

One of the first hedge fund hurdles to cross is to find out basic information on the fund itself. You need to discover who manages it, how well it has performed, how consistent it has been, and what are the terms and conditions attached to buying it. Because many of the funds are offered privately, it is not always easy to obtain contact names, phone numbers or addresses. Once you have managed it, however, the investment process is reasonably straightforward and simple.

It is important to realise that most funds operate primarily in offshore jurisdictions. The investment adviser will normally be based in some mainstream financial centre like New York, or Chicago. He has to be careful not to become so close to the fund that it could be deemed to be controlled by an onshore entity. The investment adviser technically only acts as an adviser to the investment manager, who is located in the offshore jurisdiction. So the investment adviser must be careful to distance himself from investors. In reality, the adviser is often the only decision-maker and effectively manages the fund. If he is approached, he will play a very straight bat and refer you to the fund's offshore administrator who will send out all the relevant offering documents and other information about the fund.

A useful initial source, with information on over 300 funds including names, addresses, telephone and fax numbers, contacts and a brief summary of performance, is:

The US Offshore Funds Directory
405 Park Avenue
Suite 500
New York , NY 10022
USA.
Contact: Mr. Antoine Bernheim
001 212 371 5935
001 212 758 9032 (fax)

For the most comprehensive quantitative database of hedge funds Van Hedge Fund Advisors, Inc. is unsurpassed. The company tracks a huge number of funds looking at many statistical variables and offers advanced analytical services to clients. Van Hedge can be contacted at:

Van Hedge Fund Advisors, Inc.
1608 Chickering Road
Nashville
TN 37215
USA.
Contact: Mr. George P Van, Chairman
001 615 377 2949
001 615 373 1645 (fax)

In the UK, the organisation known as TASS is a professional and friendly group with advanced information on general background, fund styles and a useful computer programme which includes a powerful performance analysis module and portfolio optimisation programme:

TASS Management Limited
27 Palace Street
London SW1E 5HW
England

Contact: Ms. Nicola Meaden
0171 233 9797
0171 233 9159 (fax)

1776 Broadway
New York, NY 10019
USA.
Contact: Ms. Karen Sampson
001 212 582 9818
001 212 582 1310 (fax)

In the US, a major source of hedge fund data and research is MAR (Managed Accounts Reports, Inc.), with an extensive database of funds and proprietary indices. It also offers a PC based asset allocation system. This group publishes a number of other products, including an excellent annual survey of performance for the industry. Details are as follows:

Managed Account Reports, Inc.
220 Fifth Avenue
19th Floor
New York, NY 10001–7781
USA.
Contact: Lydia Soto
001 212 213 6202
001 212 213 1870 (fax)

London Office
Contact: Katy Massey
0171 827 9977
0171 928 6539 (fax)

http://www.marhedge.com/mar/marhome.htm

Hedge Fund Research Inc. (HFR) publishes a quarterly journal which includes a Money Managers Forum where a roundtable group focuses on a particular investment style and participates in a Q&A session. A further section looks at investment strategies. HFR also produces its own quarterly performance indices. HFR publishes a quarterly directory of hedge funds which categorises money managers by strategy and includes contact information, background on instruments traded, total assets, inception date and monthly/quarterly and year-end performance figures:

> Hedge Fund Research, Inc
> 208 S. LaSalle
> Suite 774
> Chicago, IL 60604
> USA.
> Contact: Joseph Nicholas
> 001 312 553 6458
> 001 312 553 6461 (fax)

The two best newspapers for price information, albeit limited, are the *International Herald Tribune* and the *Financial Times*. There are, however, a number of newsletters in the US. As far as we are aware there are no publications in the UK currently.

THE INTERNET

These days nothing about accessing information is complete without comment on the Internet. There is a growing number of articles appearing and using a search motor to scan for "hedge funds" will provide you with a range of potentially interesting information, including data on the industry and individual funds.

Using the Internet is a good way of getting a feel for what is happening in the industry, particularly in the US. There is already a lot of information on the Net, and it is growing rapidly.

CHOOSING YOUR FUND(S)

Using our list of sources should make it easy to select a number of interesting funds which meet your requirements in risk/return terms. The agent or administrator for your chosen fund will provide an offering memorandum outlining the investment objectives and the terms on which it is bought and sold. Read it very carefully. Funds vary significantly in the way they are set up and operate. Scan the fine print closely, and watch especially for catches on charges or redemptions.

You should be particularly clear about how much notice you have to give before making a redemption and how soon after the redemption date you will receive your money. Check, too, whether the manager receives any special perks which you may consider unreasonable. There have been examples of a housing allowance or free air travel for the manager and his family. These examples may seem fairly far fetched, but such abuses have been recorded. Look especially at how much the fund can be geared; anything over twice should be considered carefully. The document also usually provides information on the investment managers and the key players involved together with tax and legal information.

After reading the prospectus of each fund and getting accustomed to the new jargon, the next step is to choose what to buy. Tread carefully. This is no easy task. Hedge funds vary significantly in their risk profiles and the investments they trade in. Spread your risk. It is not normally good practice to buy just one fund. A portfolio approach is far better, perhaps with a minimum of 5 investments and a maximum of 20 for a very large account.

Because of its sensitivity to the US Government's tax department, the Offshore fund industry is very careful about who it deals with, particularly US residents. Each fund provides subscription documents which ask a number of questions to satisfy the administrator that you are indeed eligible to invest in the funds and are not a US citizen. Buying Offshore funds is straightforward, but the procedure is a little different from dealing in UK unit trusts so the following check list may be helpful:

Select a fund.

Contact the administrator to obtain a prospectus.

Read the prospectus carefully, studying the small print on fees and charges, redemption procedures and minimum investment size.

Complete the application form, signing where indicated.

Fax the application form to the administrator and send the original by mail.

*If you have been introduced to the fund by a
selling agent in the UK, keep him advised on progress.
He can help ensure everything goes smoothly.*

*Arrange for monies to be telegraphically transferred to
the administrator in time to meet the subscription date,
which is usually the last day of the month or quarter.*

ASSESSING HEDGE FUNDS

We have already noted that hedge funds differ from
conventional long-only funds in that their primary aim is
to produce absolute and consistent gains irrespective of
the market background. In conventional long-only active
investment management, whether for fixed interest or
equities, it is generally considered that 80% of a
portfolio's return is related directly to the underlying
behaviour of the market. This is termed systematic risk.
In the case of fixed interest, it is known as duration. For
equities, it is beta. This leaves a mere 20% of performance
to be explained by the inherent skills of the manager,
which is termed alpha or non-systematic risk. Since only
around a quarter of unit trusts beat their benchmark
index, it is perhaps a good job that managers in the
aggregate are exposed to a mere 20% "skill" factor.

Hedge funds attempt to turn conventional
attribution figures on their head. Many funds completely
hedge out market risk and attempt only to maximise
alpha. Others do not go to such an extreme, but
nevertheless significantly reduce market risk via hedging.
They gain their returns mainly from using skill. Long-
only funds rely on capturing risk premium. The
remuneration structure of these different vehicles reflects

the size of the skill component in play. Hedge fund managers nearly always have a large profit-sharing element, receiving typically 15% to 25% of all gains, allowing them to benefit directly from using their skills to the client's advantage. They also levy a flat annual charge in addition, often 1% to 4%, although it is difficult to see how this can be justified. If the manager is sufficiently confident of his skills, he should rely solely on his performance fee. Unit trusts just charge a flat annual fee of 1% to 2% to cover expenses and make a small profit. Their main income comes from front end fees levied on sales to the public. Most hedge funds have so far avoided such a charge.

In Figure 6.2 below, the relationship between skill and reward is really brought home. Since hedge funds owe a far higher percentage of their success to the innate skills of their managers than unit trusts, it is only right that their recurring fee structure is heavily biased towards performance-related rewards. Even in falling markets, hedge funds are expected to rise. Conventional funds merely settle for losing less than the market.

	MARKET RISK Systematic Risk (%)	SKILL Non-systematic Risk (%)	MANAGER'S REWARD Annual Fee (%)	Performance Fee (%)
Unit Trust	80	20	1-2	0
Hedge Fund	20	80	1-4	15-25

Figure 6.2 The Relationship between Skill and Manager's Reward for Hedge Funds Vs Unit Trusts

In the traditional Jones model of a hedge fund, the returns are clearly down to skill. With the Soros type of

macro fund, returns are also skill based, largely because
the manager is constantly adjusting his exposure to the
markets. The **Capital Asset Pricing Model** maintains
that above-market returns are compensation for taking
undiversifiable systematic risk, but **Efficient Market
Theory** states that active managers cannot over the long
term add value. Skill managers, or at least the good ones,
therefore act against the traditional established laws of
investment by producing returns primarily through their
ability to read situations correctly rather than taking on
board capital market risk. In terms of beta or duration,
skill managers' portfolios are generally close to zero. That
should be expected since these strategies are not generally
market related. For the risk arbitrageurs, however,
because their strategies are more market correlated, beta
can rise to nearer 0.4.

Since the proliferation of funds did not start until
the late 1980s, there is not a great deal of long-term
performance data available for the industry. Specialist
indices have now been constructed, and in the future
there will be benchmarks to add more credibility to
hedge fund investing. They will also offer a more
objective way of assessing each fund against its peers.
The existing data is usually high quality, but must be
treated cautiously when drawing conclusions about
future performance, particularly when making comparison
with more traditional investments. We still do not fully
understand the behaviour of hedge funds in all
situations, and may not have yet taken on board all
aspects of their risk profile.

QUANTITATIVE ANALYSIS OF HEDGE FUNDS

Investors in long-only funds still tend to be mesmerised by absolute performance, with only the fleeting glance at risk through measuring standard deviation. In contrast, the position with hedge funds is reversed. They are more concerned with risk than with performance. Figure 6.3 below shows some of the statistical measures which are used regularly to assess hedge funds. We have shown figures for a medium risk portfolio and, where more meaningful, a range of figures. We have also included a column showing the characteristic of the underlying funds which could be included in the portfolio. Note that the individual parameters are wider, but when we combine several such funds into a portfolio, the risk-return statistics improve markedly.

INVESTMENT PARAMETERS	THE PORTFOLIO	INDIVIDUAL COMPONENT FUNDS
PERFORMANCE MEASUREMENT(%)		
Annualised geometrical return	20–24	12–33
Average 12 month rolling return	18–23	15–30
Worst 12 month rolling return	12	8
Best 12 month rolling return	28	35
Average monthly growth	2	2
CONSISTENCY MEASUREMENT (%)		
Up months	100	80–100
12 month rolling up months	100	80–100
Annualised Standard Deviation	2–4	3–8
Standard Deviation of 12 month rolling returns	2–3	2–5
RISK/DOWNSIDE ANALYSIS (%)		
Annualised Downside Deviation	0	0–10
Downside Deviation of 12 month rolling returns	0	0
Maximum Drawdown (monthly)	0	2–5
Average Drawdown	0	0–2
RISK/RETURN ANALYSIS		
Gain/Loss ratio	n/a	10
Sharpe Ratio rolling 12 month	2–4	1.5–2.5
Sortino Ratio rolling 12 month	n/a	5–1000
Average Growth/Average Drawdowns Ratio	n/a	40
Source: Argyll Investment Management Limited		

Figure 6.3 The Risk/Return Profile of a Medium Risk Hedge Fund Portfolio and the underlying funds held in it.

Not all of the terms used in Figure 6.3 are seen regularly outside hedge fund investing and so we provide below a glossary:

PERFORMANCE MEASUREMENT (%)

Annualised geometrical return – the average return each calendar year.

Average 12 month rolling return – the average return in any 12 month period.

Worst 12 month rolling return – the worst return in any 12 month period.

Best 12 month rolling return – the highest return in any 12 month period.

Average monthly growth – the average percentage rise in the portfolio over any month.

CONSISTENCY MEASUREMENT (%)

Up months – the percentage of months the portfolio has risen.

12 month rolling up months – in any 12 month period the percentage of months the portfolio has risen.

Annualised Standard Deviation – in any two years out of three, the maximum amount the performance of the portfolio would be expected to lie above or below the long-term average return, expressed as a percentage of that return.

Standard Deviation of 12 month rolling returns – as above but over any 12 month rolling period.

RISK/DOWNSIDE ANALYSIS (%)

Annualised Downside Deviation – Downside Deviation measures the probability of the portfolio returning less than the minimum acceptable return (MAR)* which is set by the investor.

Downside Deviation of 12 month rolling returns – this measures the downside deviation over any 12 rolling month period, as distinct to the annualised figure above.

Maximum Drawdown – this is the largest loss in any one month.

Average Drawdown – this is the average loss in any one month.

RISK/RETURN

Gain/Loss Ratio

$$\frac{\text{Average monthly gain x Number of up months}}{\text{Average monthly loss x Number of down months}}$$

Sharpe Ratio – Rolling 12 month

$$\frac{\text{Rolling 12 month Rate of Return–(MAR)*}}{\text{Rolling 12 month Standard Deviation}}$$

This ratio gives us a feel for the risk/return pay off – anything > 1 is acceptable and > 2 is very good.

Sortino Ratio – Rolling 12 month

$$\frac{\text{Rolling 12 month Rate of Return–(MAR)*}}{\text{Rolling 12 month Downside Deviation}}$$

*MAR is short-form for the Minimum Acceptable Return which is the lowest return an investor would be prepared to accept in return for taking risk above the risk-free rate of return. MAR normally corresponds to the yield on short-dated government bonds.

This ratio gives us an idea of the relationship between a return above the MAR and the likelihood of achieving it. The higher the figure the better.

Average Growth /Average Drawdowns Ratio –

$$\frac{\text{Average 12 month rolling return}}{\text{Average drawdown}}$$

This ratio gives us an idea of how the average drawdown affects performance. The lower this figure, the more likely we are to see sudden relatively large drops in the Net Asset Value of the fund.

QUALITATIVE ANALYSIS OF HEDGE FUNDS

Quantitative analysis can only go so far in helping us to evaluate a fund. We still need to add a component of analysis which is not so numerically based – qualitative analysis. This helps us to compare and contrast managers, even those who may have identical performance and risk profiles but very different investment approaches. It may also help us to consider if a strategy which has been successful in the past will continue to succeed in the future, and therefore whether it is appropriate to invest with a particular manager.

At the qualitative level, it is important to establish first who owns the management group, or the investment adviser, and whether it is part of a larger group or a partnership. We need to know about the senior people, their working history, and their track records. These are particularly relevant. Careful research sometimes unearths information which the principals would rather remained buried. Managers can also be analysed in terms of the types of instrument in which they invest or trade, the size of the funds they manage, and how long they have been in business. It is even worth considering, in very basic terms, whether they seem to know what they are doing. Watch also if the principals have most of their net worth in the fund, and whether they undertake to tell investors if they reduce their exposure for any reason.

Administration is critical. Offshore funds have two sets of administration to consider. At the statutory level there is the book-keeping; production of contract notes, settlement of withdrawals and timely production of Net Asset Values. At the portfolio administration level we are concerned with accurate records of trades, positions and prices.

Part of the statutory administration which you should consider is where the fund is based and who acts as administrator. In addition to tax considerations, the main reason for using an offshore base relates to investment regulations. These centres do not control and monitor investment funds as strictly as the authorities in the UK or the US. Offshore funds are free to adopt less conventional investment strategies. Investment areas which are currently popular include the Cayman Islands, the British Virgin Islands, Bermuda, the Netherlands Antilles, and Dublin. In these centres a number of well known groups now specialise in fund administration. They include MeesPierson, part of the ABN-AMRO Group, Bank of Bermuda and The International Trident Trust Group. Their role is to price the funds and keep records of shareholders, to receive new monies and pay out redemptions. The administrator is often seen as the face of the fund by investors, and his competence often forms a basis for judging the fund. Some administrators take an excessive time to produce prices each month (this being the most common pricing frequency), delaying them until nearly a month after the subscription date. Others produce prices within a week. Similar concerns over timing arise with contract notes.

In view of their complex nature, the hedge funds on average do well in maintaining all-round administration as good as that of the average UK unit trust, but there are notable exceptions. If administration is not up to scratch, or is deteriorating, it is only a matter of time before performance follows. Once the problem becomes serious the demands on management time to correct it can lead to severe underperformance.

Portfolio administration is not easy to monitor, although managers who are willing to show visiting investors their portfolios are usually on top of things. Pay attention to the quality of the back-office staff, and their qualifications. The best funds have staff educated to degree level, and may even employ some post-graduates. Often some have additional professional qualifications in the legal, accounting or actuarial fields. Dealing in such a complicated area requires highly talented people to ensure that the investment programmes run smoothly. Exact positions must be available at all times, and the staff must understand their significance so that they are able to warn managers of any impending dangers.

The quality of these unseen factors helps distinguish between funds with similar performance characteristics. If there is only space in a portfolio for one event driven manager for example, we obviously want the best. It is worth choosing the one with the best qualified personnel and slickest administration.

It is always important to take into account how

often the fund is priced, and how often it is possible to invest or redeem. Many funds deal on the last day of the month. They must receive a completed application form by this day, together with the necessary cash. Notice of redemptions varies. In most cases, the fund must be informed a few days before the end of the month. But some funds demand a full quarter's notice. Proceeds are usually sent in a few days, but sometimes they are not remitted for as much as two, or even three, months. As a general rule never underestimate the dangers of poor administration.

SAFE CUSTODY – PRIME BROKER

Owing to the complexity of some funds and the various instruments they trade, they have found it easier to deal with one head broker. Balancing long and short positions can be best achieved with the help of a central processing facility. Without this, hedge funds could not easily finance their long positions from their short ones. The prime broker, normally a major broking house, therefore acts as the coordinator of all trade, including taking care of settlement and the custody of securities. It does not necessarily undertake all trades, since these are often carried out by execution-only brokers who report back to the prime broker and to the hedge fund with details of trades, but look to the prime broker for settlement. It is wise to ensure that the prime broker is well known and of substance, since it acts in a pivotal position in the success of the fund.

In Table 6.4, on pages 154–156, we show a typical Qualitative Analysis Sheet which lists the corporate, administrative and principal aspects of a fund. This one is for Infinity Investors. It contains the minimum information which investors need before deciding on a purchase. It does not include qualitative information on the investment style of the manager, which must be analysed separately in conjunction with the quantitative performance data for the fund. All of the features must be considered carefully, since these skill-based investments are different from conventional asset types and carry specific and new risks.

INFINITY INVESTORS LIMITED

Registered Address:	Mailing Address:
Infinity Investors Ltd	Infinity Investors Ltd
Memorial Square	c/o Trident Trust Company (Cayman) Ltd
P.O. Box 556	One Capital Place
Charleston, Nevis	P.O. Box 847
West Indies	Grand Cayman
	Cayman Islands, B.W.I.

Administrator:

Trident Trust Company (Cayman) Limited
One Capital Place
P.O. Box 847
Grand Cayman
Cayman Islands, B.W.I.

Trident contact: Rick Gorter   Tel. 001 809 949 0880

Fax. 001 809 949 0881

Other Fund Details	
Inception	January 1994
Minimum Investment	US$ 1 million
Subscription Date	Subscriptions monthly
Withdrawals	Funds invested may first be withdrawn 12 months after the date of the original investment. After that funds may be withdrawn at the end of any month. For any withdrawal to occur the company must receive notice 60 days in advance.
Financial Year	31 December
Fund Size	US$ 60 million
Structure	Limited international business company
Place of Incorporation	British West Indies
Manager of the fund	Suisse Finance Corporation
Total funds under management	US$ 270 million
Background of main People	Clark Hunt worked as an analyst at Goldman Sachs and was involved in financial transactions with an aggregate value in excess of US$ 1 billion. These transactions included mergers, acquisitions, initial public offerings, cross currency swaps and leveraged buy-outs.
	Barrett Wissman attended Yale University and graduated with a degree in economics and politics. Mr Wissman joined Lazard Freres & Co where he worked in the international mergers and acquisitions and the international project finance departments. In 1987, Mr Wissman assumed the role of CEO of Athena Products Corporation in which his family owns a majority interest. In addition Mr Wissman manages the family's portfolio of domestic and international equities, derivatives, bonds and currencies.

Manager invests in fund	Yes
Administrator	Trident Trust Company (Cayman) Limited
Auditors	KPMG Peat Marwick
Prime Broker	
Custodian	Barclays Bank PLC
E&OE.	

Table 6.4 Qualitative Analysis Sheet – Infinity Investors

The above table answers many of the basic non investment qualitative questions which should be considered when assessing a manager. The list is not exhaustive. If possible, it is best to meet the people who manage the funds face to face. This is growing easier, as a number of US managers now come to the UK frequently.

MONITORING

All funds must be monitored closely as an ongoing exercise. One of the greatest dangers to guard against is holding funds which invest simultaneously using gearing and illiquid positions. This is the latter day equivalent of the old adage "Never borrow short and lend long". If the game changes in the market place, these funds can be very exposed in a downturn. Unless the managers are completely on top of things, they will face heavy losses. The most important thing to establish is whether the manager has adequate risk control measures in place, whether they reflect the nature of the strategy he is following, and whether he is monitoring his portfolio diligently. Pay special attention to any change of manager. Why is he leaving? Who is his replacement and what experience does he have? So often a change of manager can lead to a marked deterioration in performance. Somehow, it produces an improvement less frequently.

As the use of personal computers has increased, so has the ability to monitor funds more successfully. Now it is possible to make use of a valuable analytical tool by monitoring the relationship between risk and return over time. A monthly plot of the 12 month rolling return of a fund against its standard deviation can build into a fascinating picture. It is useful because it measures the risk/return pattern over time, and monitors any change in this relationship. That could be due, for instance, to the manager changing his investment style, or perhaps to opportunities for a given strategy diminishing. It is an early warning signal that things are changing, for the better or for the worse. Figure 6.5 below shows an example of such a chart.

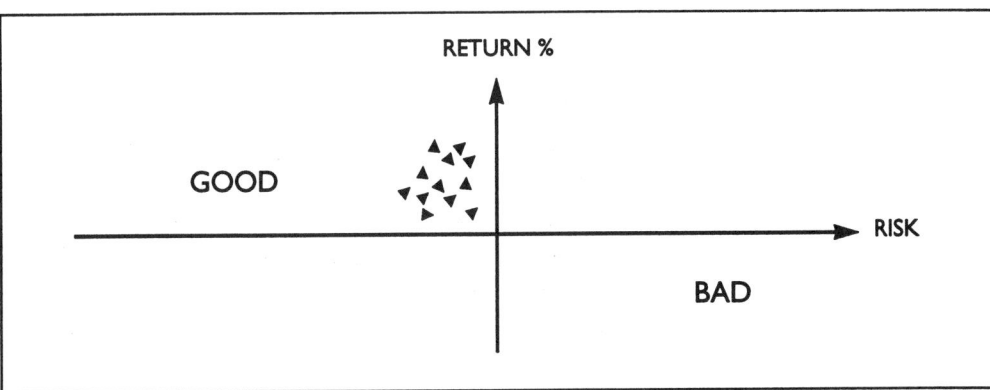

Figure 6.5 The Risk/Return Monitor

The noticeable thing about the chart is the consistency of returns this imaginary fund has achieved, and the very small variation in its dynamics. This pattern suggests a well managed fund. If performance were deteriorating, the points on the chart would move downwards towards the horizontal axis. If, however, the manager were taking more risk, perhaps in an attempt to recover from a period of poor performance, the points would move to the right, indicating increasing volatility. A move to the bottom right hand quarter would not be good news, and would indicate falling returns and increasing risk levels. If this should happen, the fund should generally be sold. An improving trend emerges when the points move towards the top left hand quarter, representing improving performance and falling volatility.

FUND OF FUNDS

For many private investors and institutions, the effort required to monitor their investments adequately is too great a burden. It is more sensible for such investors to buy a multi-manager fund where the manager acts as an asset allocator and spreads the fund's monies across a number of hedge funds which he selects. Such a fund depends on the skill of the manager to undertake the necessary due diligence on the components of the portfolio. Even so, investors must undertake some investigation themselves to make sure that the fund of fund's manager knows what he is doing. Once again, this can be achieved partly through quantitative analysis of previous results and through a qualitative assessment of the skills and resources employed to select individual managers.

The essential structure is very straightforward, as shown in Figure 6.6 below:

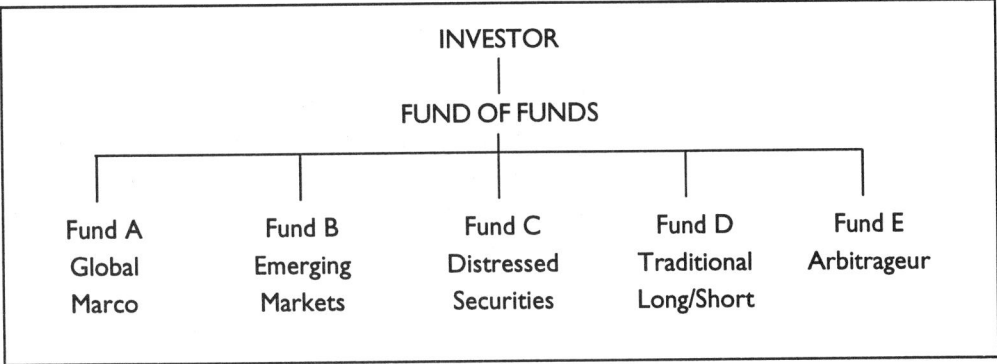

Figure 6.6 Fund of Funds – the essential structure

Fund of funds vary considerably in their investment styles, like the underlying hedge funds in which they invest. Essentially an investor in one of these funds needs to know two pieces of information:

What is the manager's investment style?
How is this implemented?

There are a few recognised strategies which revolve around:

Maximum return achievable – here the manager goes all out for high performance and concentrates on sectors which offer the best returns. This can produce volatile returns, and is not a prudent path, although the results can be very good.

Target return – it is less risky to invest with a manager who sets a target return and is not motivated to take large bets. Target returns normally fall in the 13% to 20% pa. bracket and are achieved through a well diversified portfolio of funds pursuing varied strategies.

Specific sector strategies – the manager will concentrate on a given recognised sector strategy, perhaps emerging markets or risk arbitrage, and construct a dedicated portfolio consisting of funds specialising only in that strategy.

Using the fund of funds route provides the investor with the opportunity to gain exposure to a greater number of strategies than might be possible by buying individual funds. It overcomes the problems which might be posed by insufficient money to meet the minimum entry requirements for individual funds, lack of knowledge and information on the opportunities available, or the lack of sufficient experience to blend funds into a sensible and coherent portfolio.

There are so many funds today that it is impossible for most investors to monitor each one and select only the best. It requires a professional approach and time and effort to do a thorough job. Fund of funds managers supply this, and undertake the research and strategic assessment required to keep the risk of failure within acceptable limits. They also help by spreading risk over a number of funds, thus tending to produce more consistent results than an individual could achieve with fewer investments.

There are drawbacks. Investors pay an additional set of fees, which usually amount to around 1% to 2% pa. Sometimes there may be a small incentive fee on top. This is no problem with a good manager, but not all managers are experienced or necessarily talented at picking winning managers. And sometimes, fund of funds vehicles are less liquid than individual accounts. There is a practical reason for this. If a manager receives a redemption, he may have to sell some investments. These investments themselves may not be liquid, and he must wait for the proceeds before he can satisfy his own investors.

On balance, the fund of funds route offers investors a sensible way into hedge fund investing, and is a logical first step. More consistent returns should be expected with lower aggregate volatility than in the underlying investments.

Individually or through fund of funds, hedge funds offer advantages over traditional investments and warrant a place in most portfolios. Problems in obtaining adequate information can be surmounted through some of the sources in this chapter. Analysing hedge funds requires different skills from those used in assessing conventional investments but the potential returns are well worth the effort. And hedge fund investing is fun. It offers investors an insight into strategies which are thought provoking and exciting. In comparison to buying BP and selling Shell, going long of Turkish Treasury Bills and hedging the Lira is far more stimulating – and it can be more profitable.

Although the opportunities are considerable, the watchword must nevertheless be caution. Do not run before you can walk. If you do not understand what you are doing, hedge funds can be dangerous.

CONSTRUCTING A BALANCED PORTFOLIO OF HEDGE FUNDS

In all investment, the key to success lies in the structure and the management of the portfolio. A well considered, planned, executed, and monitored portfolio will produce far better long term results than one put together in haste and left to roll on unsupervised.

We should look to reach our target level of return, while keeping risk to a minimum. Constructing the parameters of a hedge fund portfolio is no different to creating an equity portfolio, although the underlying analysis is more complex. The major issues are:

- Defining the primary investment objectives.

- Establishing an investment policy to meet those objectives.

- Analysing and selecting, using quantitative and qualitative methods, the most suitable funds in which to invest.

- Measuring the correlation between component funds.

- Optimising the portfolio.

- Qualitative issues.

- Re-analysis. Making the final selection of funds to include in the portfolio.

- Monitoring and analysing the chosen funds continuously and considering possible substitutes.

DEFINING THE
PRIMARY INVESTMENT OBJECTIVES

The most important aspect at the outset is to determine what is to be achieved. This should be clearly set out in terms of:

- Minimum acceptable rate of return.

- Maximum acceptable standard deviation of return.

- Maximum permissible rolling 12 month loss.

- Minimum proportion of up months.

- Downside deviation of 12 month rolling returns.

- Acceptable Sharpe Ratio.

- Acceptable Sortino Ratio.

- Acceptable investment styles.

- Level of acceptable liquidity in the portfolio.

We can usually agree on the quantitative measures of performance fairly comfortably. In general terms, against a background of 3% to 4% inflation, an annual return of around 15% to 20% is attractive for a medium-risk portfolio. It means that the investments will double every four to five years. Some investors may prefer to forgo some return in exchange for less volatility and more consistency.

Towards the lower end of returns, 10% to 13% is still attractive in a low-risk environment, and should be attainable consistently. At the other end of the scale, 35% annual returns are obviously ambitious, but may be attained using a futures based strategy. That would require the investor to accept high volatility.

Quantitative risk measures are more difficult to set. Volatility, the proportion of up months, and the level of maximum permitted losses are important, and yield an insight into how much risk the investor is prepared to tolerate. Anyone who is uncomfortable losing money over a 12 month period should not invest in any portfolio above the medium-risk level – even this may be too near the limit for some. Experience shows that it is prudent always to err towards the lower risk strategies, and to guard against being seduced by juicier returns, if the investor has a powerful aversion to losing money.

Downside deviation, the Sharpe Ratio and Sortino Ratio are less emotional measures of the portfolio's characteristics, and tell us more about its construction in terms of efficiency. These measures put the icing on the cake and if sensible values are set, help to secure the quality of the portfolio.

The issue of what investments may be acceptable is particularly relevant to institutional investors such as pension funds or insurance companies. They may be concerned about certain asset types appearing in their portfolios, from both a marketing and investment standpoint. The use of commodity based trading funds can send a shiver up many people's backs, and is obviously unwelcome for some. If you are a private investor, never invest in any strategies you do not understand, particularly high-risk ones.

Equally never overlook the importance of liquidity. Many investors, private or institutional, view liquidity as a type of risk attribute in itself. If an investment is not readily realisable, quite rightly it tends to be perceived as potentially dangerous. In conventional investment, stocks with a small capitalisation are often very illiquid. If the market falls, they cannot be sold for love nor money. This can be a most frustrating and costly experience. Institutional investors recognise this more than most, but understand that if the rest of the portfolio is highly liquid, it should not be a problem. Pension and insurance funds rarely have to raise liquidity to meet their long-term liabilities. But private investors may take a shorter view. Liquidity is all about money in the hand for them, and they may be frightened to be told that cash from sales will not be available for some weeks. It is important to recognise and understand the significance of liquidity from the moment any portfolio is put together.

ESTABLISHING AN INVESTMENT POLICY

Investors can be divided into three main categories; low, medium and high risk. Establishing a model portfolio for each type at an early stage helps to put each onto the right shelf, but not necessarily into the correct pigeon hole. In Figure 7.1 below, we show the major characteristics in examples of each of these portfolios, to offer an insight into the character and the variability of their historic returns and risk profiles.

STATISTIC	LOW RISK	MEDIUM RISK	HIGH RISK
PERIOD	30.9.93–31.1.96	30.9.92–31.1.96	31.10.92–31.1.96
PERFORMANCE MEASUREMENT (%)			
Annualised geometric return	13.59	22.99	41.08
Average 12 month rolling return	14.31	22.35	45.24
Worst 12 month rolling return	12.07	13.39	22.94
Best 12 month rolling return	15.96	28.76	87.07
VOLATILITY ANALYSIS (%)			
Up months	100.00	100.00	67.50
12 month rolling up months	100.00	100.00	100.00
Annualised Standard Deviation	2.90	3.68	23.33
Standard Deviation of 12 month rolling returns	1.20	2.70	15.12
Maximum Drawdown	0.00	0.00	10.94
Average of 5 worst drawdowns	0.00	0.00	4.50
RISK/RETURN ANALYSIS			
Sharpe Ratio rolling 12 month	8.69	3.65	2.74
Sortino Ratio rolling 12 month	n/a	n/a	n/a

Source: Argyll Investment Management Limited

Figure 7.1 The Attributes of Low, Medium and High-Risk Hedge Fund Portfolios – A Statistical Analysis

ANALYSING AND SELECTING FUNDS

Once the outline of the desired portfolio has been set, we can analyse potential investments. A low-risk portfolio should be directed towards funds which have very small standard deviations of return and high consistency. As a result, they will have fairly modest performances. Most such funds will be pursuing a heavily hedged strategy, giving up some potential gains as an insurance premium to hedge out downside risk. There will be only a relatively narrow range of managers following these policies. They will probably be those adopting low-risk arbitrage strategies. Alternatively they may be trend traders, only looking to take a small return from each trade with good stop-loss cover in place.

For the high-risk portfolio, we need to direct more attention towards the risk takers. They may be trading leveraged positions in futures and commodities, with big positions in high-risk, high return investments.

The medium-risk portfolio is an amalgam of the two approaches, and may contain the odd investment held by each. This portfolio aims to balance the risk-return levels. It discards very low-risk funds where potential returns are too low. Equally, it fights shy of funds where the risk is too high, despite potentially attractive returns.

The construction process involves a number of steps:

- Scanning the database for funds with suitable risk/return characteristics.

- Analysing suitable funds in terms of inter-correlations and selecting perhaps the 10 best fitting funds from a combination of quantitative and qualitative analysis.

- Re-analysis of the portfolio to confirm its attributes meet the target.

- Substitution of a fund(s) to enhance the portfolio's required characteristics.

In selecting the building blocks, we identify the most suitable funds by screening our database, searching for funds with appropriate risk/return attributes which complement the characteristics of our desired portfolio.

For example, for a medium-risk portfolio of 10 equally weighted funds, we would look for the portfolio and funds to fall within the investment parameters in Figure 7.2 below:

INVESTMENT PARAMETERS	THE PORTFOLIO	INDIVIDUAL COMPONENT FUNDS
Av 12 month rolling return (%)	18–25	15-30
Standard Deviation of 12 month rolling (%)	2–3	2–5
Downside Deviation of 12 month rolling (%)	0	0
Maximum Drawdown (monthly) (%)	0	2–5
Sharpe Ratio	3–4	1.5–2.5
Sortino Ratio	n/a	5–1000
Source: Argyll Investment Management Limited		

Figure 7.2 Investment Parameters.

Although the parameters for the fund and portfolio are the same, the ranges permitted for individual funds are larger than those of the portfolio. This is because of the expected portfolio effect which will occur when individual funds with low correlations are combined to form a portfolio. The component characteristic of each fund will cancel each other out to a degree, creating lower risk but lower return characteristics for the overall portfolio.

After scanning our database, let us suppose we find 12 suitable candidates with acceptable quantitative and qualitative attributes. Next we must see how they fit together. By changing the mix of the 12 funds, we can arrive at a best-fit portfolio. Then it is important to ensure that the funds we have selected have well diversified characteristics when compared against each other.

THE CORRELATION PROCESS

A correlation programme can be used to produce a matrix of coefficients of correlation for a combination of any two funds. This measures the degree of similarity in behaviour which can be expected between the pair. In brief, a result of 1 indicates that the two funds will have identical behaviour, 0 indicates there will be no statistical relationship at all, while –1 indicates that the pair are perfectly negatively correlated ie. if one is rising, the other is falling. By comparing each possible pairing, we can generate a correlation matrix which allows us to look at each fund and see how it correlates to the others in the portfolio. In this way, we can select the funds with the lowest correlations, and create a portfolio with the highest level of diversification.

This allows us to avoid creating a portfolio which has inbuilt biases, such as a heavy weighting in funds correlated to the S&P 500 Index. By monitoring the correlations of each component part, we can ensure that the portfolio is well diversified, and is unlikely to be unduly influenced by changes in one specific market trend. This should generate much more consistent returns, with lower standard deviations.

We can include any market indices we choose in the correlation matrix to see how the funds relate to them. In similar fashion, we can measure the correlation of the final portfolio against various markets. This can be very helpful, particularly if we are specifically designing a portfolio which we want to be uncorrelated to a given market.

In Figure 7.3 below we show a typical correlation matrix for a medium-risk portfolio.

FUNDS	A	B	C	D	E	F	G
A	1.0						
B	0.1159	1.0					
C	–0.1039	–0.2214	1.0				
D	0.0991	0.2775	–0.3092	1.0			
E	–0.2995	–0.3266	0.1668	–0.6177	1.0		
F	–0.2492	0.2088	–0.1163	0.1623	–0.2872	1.0	
G	0.4991	0.2337	–0.2026	0.3023	–0.0972	0.0476	1.0

Source: Argyll Investment Management Limited

Figure 7.3 A Typical Correlation Matrix for a Medium-Risk Portfolio.

We do not hold a pair of funds where the inter-correlation is greater than 0.4. If this were to occur, we would replace the fund which has the highest correlation with the other funds. For example, in the above matrix we would replace fund G since it has a correlation of 0.4991 with fund A. We would replace it in preference to A since it is more heavily correlated to the other funds than A. By ensuring that the highest correlation reached in the matrix is 0.4 or below, we can be fairly certain that we have a well diversified portfolio which should exhibit quite low standard deviations.

When correlations average around 0.2, the gains from diversification and the reduction of risk become modest after adding more than 10 managers. So, as a very rough rule of thumb, investors should look to build portfolios with at least 10 managers, but should ensure that the average intercorrelations are 0.2 or below.

OPTIMISATION

It is possible to optimise a hedge fund portfolio by varying weightings to achieve the best theoretical risk/return measures, but there are problems. Unfortunately, the lack of sufficient historical data on how hedge funds perform over time makes it unwise to risk allocating a high weighting to individual funds. For example, in the years to 1994, most funds performed well. Those operating in the apparently low-risk, leveraged bond arbitrage areas showed exceptional returns with low variance. But in 1994, some of these funds had a difficult time as their underlying assets became illiquid, and slumped in value. Indeed, many funds were not hedged at all. Sceptics would claim that they were just riding blindly on the falling interest rate cycle. In such circumstances, a geared fund can be wiped out quickly, as we saw with the Askin Capital Management's Granite Fund. Gearing can produce excellent returns, but it carries greater risks than many managers realise. It is always crucial to assess whether the different managers are using skill, or merely gambling.

As we have seen, in theory hedge fund returns come from capturing alpha (non-systematic risk) through skill, rather than earning the economic risk premium associated with market risk. This is a vital distinction, and it is the underlying difference in philosophy between long-only investing and hedge funds.

The "total risk" concept can be equally applied to individual shares or hedge funds. Both offer the potential to fail and become worthless. For a reasonably diversified portfolio of shares and hedge funds the risk and consequence of a complete failure is reduced to virtually zero. Nevertheless, within the portfolio one share or hedge fund may still fail. For a conventional long-only institutional equity portfolio, since the correlations between the individual components are usually quite high, a relatively large number of shares (around 20) are needed to diversify non-systematic risk. For a hedge fund portfolio fewer funds (around 10) are needed because of the generally lower correlations encountered.

Leaving aside the diversification arguments, for the average institution, the chance of a blow-up would make it imprudent to have less than 10 holdings in a designated hedge fund-only portfolio. The private individual might be forced by the limit on his available funds to accept the higher risk inherent in a portfolio of perhaps five holdings. Consequently there may be little point trying to optimise the portfolio if cash constraints inhibit a proper spread. Nevertheless, it may still be useful to run an unconstrained optimisation model. It may throw up some interesting figures which will alert the manager to the specific attributes of various funds. If, for example, one fund dominates the model, this will prove to have very peculiar characteristics. If another should fail to qualify for inclusion or warrant at best only a small representation, perhaps it could be replaced with a better alternative.

QUALITATIVE ISSUES

When the overall parameters of the portfolio have been set, and the potential funds selected, it is necessary to assess all of their qualitative characteristics. We should ensure that the funds have complementary styles, and that we have not included any biases into the portfolio. Any such clashes or bias must be addressed and neutralised by changing some of the funds.

RE-ANALYSIS OF THE PORTFOLIO

After concluding the qualitative and the quantitative analysis, we must check if the portfolio as a whole will produce the desired risk and return features. Recalculate the various statistical measures using an equally weighted portfolio. If the performance and risk characteristics still meet our objectives, we have found the solution. If not, we must alter some of the components to increase performance or reduce risk. It may be impossible to construct our target portfolio from the funds at our disposal. In this case, there is nothing for it but to choose less demanding parameters.

MONITORING

It is impossible to achieve good results without monitoring all of the portfolio's investments continuously. The individual risk attributes and performance of each fund must be analysed to ensure they continue to be acceptable, and the inter-correlations of the component parts of the portfolio should be scrutinised constantly. If there is any variation from expectations, it should be examined closely. It may be necessary to replace one fund with a more suitable candidate. There should be a thorough analysis at least once a quarter.

HEDGE FUND PORTFOLIOS COMPARED TO TRADITIONAL PORTFOLIOS

In Figure 7.2 on page 169, the medium-risk portfolio is tightly defined by risk and return parameters, with a greater emphasis on risk than return. This is unlike traditional portfolios, which are more loosely defined with an accent more on returns. If the portfolio consists of bonds and equities, the manager will control the perceived risk by adjusting the holding of fixed interest investments. He will add bonds to reduce risk, and reduce them to increase risk. But by way of risk, he only considers standard deviation, certainly not downside deviation. By comparison, hedge fund investing is far more sophisticated. We really can start to quantify the expected returns and the associated risks in terms of not only volatility, but also of failure to reach the Minimum Acceptable Return. Right from the start, hedge fund investors know what to expect, and know the likelihood of failure.

It is possible to optimise a portfolio of traditional and hedge fund investments using conventional mean variance techniques (see Chapter 4) to produce the mix with the lowest risk for a given level of expected performance. Although there is a great deal of data on hedge funds, it is sparse and relatively recent by comparison with data on equities, bonds and cash. Since the majority of returns from conventional and hedge funds come from two different sources, market risk versus alpha, it is questionable whether combining the data in the same model can produce sensible results.

As we discussed in Chapter 4 on **Post Modern Portfolio Theory,** hedge funds have two outstanding characteristics:

- They have low correlations with traditional asset classes.

- They offer high expected risk adjusted returns.

Returns from hedge funds are achieved primarily by skill. If we dismiss the theoretical notion that this is not possible on an extended basis, since all returns regress to the mean, adding hedge funds to a diversified conventional institutional portfolio should lead to much better risk-adjusted returns. But because of their superior risk/return characteristics, hedge funds will always come to dominate mean-variance optimisation programmes to the exclusion of traditional asset classes.

Since such optimisations do not include alpha data, their results could be questionable. However, alpha is a very powerful commodity. Positive alpha is a risk free gain and will always be accorded more value than any beta which carries market risk. In addition, alpha is usually uncorrelated with other asset classes and has lower volatility. Hence optimising using alpha data would favour hedge funds more than conventional investments.

Optimising a portfolio which seeks to combine conventional investments with hedge funds, unless constrained, will become very heavily weighted towards hedge funds. This would probably be unacceptable since investors are still not accustomed to the use of these vehicles they may feel exposed to risks as yet unknown. In a mixed hedge/conventional portfolio, irrespective of theory, hedge funds should probably at present not represent more than 30% of total assets. There is no theoretical reason for a 30% limit and as time passes the figure may well rise as investors become more at ease with the use of these funds. Much the same behaviour has been seen in UK pension fund portfolios in the past 40 years as the percentage held in gilts has fallen from over 50% to nearer 10% while equities have increased from around 25% to 75% reflecting their better risk/return characteristics.

Simple caution should not mask the very real attractions of hedge funds. Using them on their own, or in combination with traditional assets, provides investors with the opportunity to define their dream portfolio in terms of risk and reward. Barring bad luck, it should produce worthwhile results.

ARE HEDGE FUNDS SUITABLE FOR ALL INVESTORS?

Almost all investors should give serious consideration to the inclusion of some hedge funds in their portfolios.

Their emphasis on skill and on measuring risk gives them significant advantages. Unfortunately, they are trapped in a morass of popular misconceptions which prompt most advisers to suggest that investors steer well clear of these "high-risk punting funds". In truth, this flawed advice is only appropriate to a small section of the hedge fund industry. Because the whole movement is damned by such an inaccurate generalisation, and dogged by the cult of the individual, investors are missing out on some great opportunities.

It cannot be repeated too often – hedge funds can be distinguished from traditional equity or bond portfolios by their accent on absolute returns and risk management. Equity and bond investors are relative investors, aiming to beat their relevant index, but without necessarily being committed to producing a positive return. Merely by beating their allocated benchmark, they can claim to have succeeded, irrespective of how much money they have made or lost. But as we all know, absolute liabilities cannot be paid out of relative gains. Hedge managers only count success in terms of money gained. Relative returns are irrelevant. When world markets are rising gently, the returns from medium-risk hedge funds and traditional equity investments are likely to be similar, even on a risk-adjusted basis.

When world equity markets are shuffling sideways or retreating, the picture changes sharply. Then traditional funds find it very hard to make real returns for their investors, and all of the risk is on the downside. That is not true of hedge funds. They can employ a whole range of strategies to allow them to profit from sluggish or falling markets. Arbitrage, and even event-driven strategies are all market neutral, and do not rely for their success on any particular trend in the market. If we could be certain that we were about to enter a slow growth economic environment, or a period when equities or bonds were likely to underperform, we would undoubtedly be better building up exposure to hedge funds.

As we saw in Chapter 5 Figure 5.1 on page 120, hedge funds have significantly outstripped traditional bonds and equities in terms of higher performance and lower risk.

This graph strongly suggests that hedge funds have a legitimate place in investors' portfolios and are now a serious asset class. Nevertheless, it is difficult to classify their position exactly, since compared to conventional assets the spread of risk and reward across the various strategies is very large.

WHO ARE THE POTENTIAL INVESTORS?

Individuals, trusts, foundations and endowment funds in the US, and to a lesser extent in Switzerland, have been the major investors in hedge funds to date. They have been less constrained by restrictive legislation, and keener to search out superior new investments. By and large, their entrepreneurial streak has been well rewarded. In the future the net will widen and many more investors from various centres will move into this rapidly expanding market.

PRIVATE INDIVIDUALS

Private individuals have been the main driving force in expanding the industry. A number of wealthy families, able to make their own decisions without reference to a number of advisers, have supplied the seed corn to back new managers in the hope of realising good returns. Indeed, in the US many hedge funds have been started primarily to manage the assets of just one family.

As more private investors and their advisers become aware of the benefits hedge funds offer, a growing number will use them. These investors are perhaps the most sensitive to volatility, and are attracted by the idea of consistent returns.

If hedge funds continue to offer better risk/return patterns than conventional unit trusts, the traditional savings industry in the UK will come under pressure. The process will accelerate as specialist funds begin to set up in the UK to concentrate on shares and bonds. As we have already seen with the Egerton European Fund, successful long-only UK investment managers can make the transition to hedge fund management.

There are a great many talented investors in the City of London. It is just a matter of time before more of them set up their own funds. Initially they will probably receive funding from larger, more established managers, just as Egerton did. There are large personal benefits available to the managers who strike out on their own, and the more entrepreneurial and talented should have few problems in making their mark. The new funds should find a ready and willing market among private investors as more objective reporting of hedge funds emerges.

The catalyst necessary to speed up this process is an expanding group of knowledgeable professional advisers. They will help private investors to enter this market, either by managing discretionary portfolios or offering advisory services. These new specialists will effectively act as hedge fund brokers, advising on the relative attractions of different funds to suit different investment objectives. In the US, such advisers are already generating big business.

PENSION FUNDS

In 1908 Lloyd George introduced his 25p a week pension, but this was only available following a Means Test and could only be paid to men and women over the age of 70. It was not until the National Insurance Act of 1946 that membership of the State pension scheme became a requirement for all employees.

The history of the occupational pension scheme dates back to the end of the last century when the railway companies, banks and insurance offices became the first private sector pension providers. In the early days the schemes were nearly all non-contributory and mainly for senior personnel only. The granting of tax exemptions to self-invested pension funds following the First World War produced the catalyst for growth, although this was slowed somewhat by the economic climate of the 1920s and 1930s and of course the Second World War. It was not really until the 1940s and 1950s that real progress occurred. Since then there has been an explosion in these schemes and the monies invested by them so that today the industry has more than £470 billion invested on its behalf.

The investment side of the UK pension fund industry is dominated by the actuaries and the major investment houses. Their traditional approach coupled with the natural caution of the trustees, who have come under increasing legislative and fiduciary pressure, has exerted a degree of inertia over the evolution of investment thinking. The inclusion of new asset types into portfolios has been constrained partly through fear of the business risks associated with new investments. The smaller investment firms have tended to support new investment concepts first. Where these have led to superior returns, others have eventually followed. The increasing percentage held in overseas investments by the median pension scheme might be a good example here.

Initially, pension fund investments were largely confined to gilts. There were few equities, since they were perceived to be too high risk, too volatile. In the 1950s this approach was turned on its head by the writings and actions of the manager of the Imperial Tobacco Pension Scheme, Ross Goobey. He reasoned that equities as a long-term investment were far from high risk, but instead provided one of the few ways to be reasonably sure of gaining real returns after inflation. It is worth recalling how earth-shattering this idea was. Until 1955, the yield on UK equities had always been higher than on gilts. That reflected the view that equities were high-risk investments, and should offer a premium yield as compensation. The high global economic growth of the 1960s partly fuelled by the war in Vietnam led to strong gains in UK equities and rising earnings and dividends. Although UK equity yields remained stable across this period, gilt yields rose from 5.6% to 8.5%.

From this point onwards investors began to talk of the reverse yield gap.

Between January 1950 and December 1959, UK gilts fell in real terms by –3.2% pa. On the other hand UK equities rose on average by a real 12.9% pa. At the same time, the final salary pension scheme was being introduced across much of industry in Britain and America. This put the onus of supplying a pension more firmly onto the employer, away from the employee. Since the amount the employer had to find to fund the scheme was directly related to its performance, it was not long before performance came under the spotlight. Performance is crucial to funding. For each 1% of added annual performance, long-term funding can be reduced by roughly 20%. As thinking developed in the late 1950s, a more critical view of traditional investing emerged.

Led by Ross Goobey, the cult of the equity took off in the UK. This was good for the long-term returns of pension funds, and it provided a new business opportunity for the merchant banks. Because of close connections on the corporate finance side, many of them had secured the investment mandate for company pension funds, albeit not at particularly attractive rates of remuneration. They had found it hard to charge a lot for managing a gilt portfolio. Some claim that investment management was almost offered as a loss leader, rather than a business in its own right. While the merchant banks were waking up to the opportunities, the insurance companies who had quite large client bases at the smaller end of the market, were slow to react. They did not move into equities so quickly, and lost out to the merchant banks who saw that managing portfolios which included equities allowed them to charge much higher fees.

Although inflation was to be the spur towards larger equity positions, throughout the 1950s and 1960s it remained rather benign, here and in the US. Consequently real equity returns were exceptionally good. In the 1950s UK inflation was around 3.5% and in the 1960s 4.2%. Real average annual returns for UK equities and gilts over the 20 year period were 8.4% and –2.6% respectively. This staggering difference in returns made more people raise the equity exposure of their own pension funds or trusts. With such good returns, fees and competition increased. The merchant banks began to realise that their investment departments were real money spinners. With low capital employed and high returns, they were good businesses and many more players entered the market.

In the US, in particular, people started leaving the big organisations to set up on their own, creating the new breed of money managers so common today. A similar move did not reach the UK until the 1980s.

The shift in asset allocation towards equities was nevertheless a slow process, here and in the US, partly because there was a setback in equity markets just as it was gathering momentum. In 1964 and again in 1966, the FT Actuaries Index fell by over 10%. This was followed by rip-roaring bull markets. They terminated in the 1973-74 crash, when the Index fell by over 70% from top to bottom. Such movements reminded people that equities can be far more volatile than gilts over short periods. The subsequent oil crises in the 1970s triggered bursts of inflation which gave the final impetus to equities, and established them rather than gilts as the premier pension fund investment.

The average UK pension fund has changed its asset allocation markedly over time. Since 1980, the percentage held in gilts has fallen significantly, while the overseas element has grown massively, largely as a result of the abolition of the dollar premium in 1979. Meanwhile UK equity holdings have increased from around 45% to 54%, a rise of 20%.

	31.12.80 %		31.12.95 %
Gilts		21	10
Overseas bonds		n/a	4
Equities		54	77
UK	45		54
Overseas	9		23
Property		20	5
Cash		5	4
TOTAL		100	100

Source: The WM Company

Figure 8.1 The Changing Asset Allocation of UK Pension Funds: 1980–95.

The US developed a little differently, owing to the imposition of ERISA legislation in 1974. This came into place at the depth of the worst equity market collapse since the Great Depression, and was introduced to protect pension scheme assets by laying down rules and regulations for the industry. The Act was hard-hitting and effectively gave pension trustees little choice but to stick to US bonds and equities.

This legislation is probably one of the main reasons why even today the US pension industry has only 7% of the assets it manages invested overseas. The heavy domestic emphasis also reflects the fact that the 1980s were such a good period for US equities and bonds, with annual gains of 18% and 13% respectively, that there was no real incentive to go further afield, even though the EAFE index returned a phenomenal 22% during the decade. Some catch-up in US pension fund foreign investment did, however, take place and the overseas content edged up from around 2% in 1980 to 7% today. That is still a far cry from the UK pension fund's average overseas weighting of 27% in 1995.

Institutional investors like pension fund trustees are not, surprisingly and contrary to common belief, in the performance business. They set internal minimum rates of return. If these are attained, they ensure that the schemes are properly funded and will be able to pay present and future pension obligations after allowing for new contributions and any inflation escalation clauses. This hurdle is 4% to 5% annually above the rate of inflation. In recent years we have seen exceptional returns, by historic measures, from the Anglo-Saxon stockmarkets against a background of moderate to falling inflation and low interest rates. The pension funds have therefore easily achieved their required actuarial returns and have perhaps turned their attentions too far towards absolute performance returns. Trustees have become obsessed with their position in the performance tables. In the eyes of the company finance director, who is often a trustee, performance is everything.

Pension fund trustees need only be reasonably certain that the assets of the fund have been prudently diversified. It is not necessary to prove that an overseas component is a prerequisite, particularly if all is going well at home. The trustees know that if the fund returns a real rate of around 5% pa. on a consistent basis, the actuarial scope of the assets is probably going to cover the pensioners' needs. If, however, the real return on assets fell to just 3%, a long-term problem would be building up. Following the phenomenal returns for pension fund assets over the last 20 years of 15.2% pa. – especially during the 1980s when markets readjusted from a period of high inflation to one of deflation – we may have seen the best of returns for some time.

Surely as night follows day, the next secular move will not be towards deflation, but back toward inflation and the de-rating of equities and higher yields on bonds. This could alter the current value of pension schemes assets. More importantly, it would affect the underlying actuarial assumptions of returns and require a higher rate of funding if the trustees do not act to find alternative investments to boost returns.

If we are heading towards a period of lower returns, a review of the median pension fund's asset mix is needed urgently. We know that over the long term, bonds barely offer a real return. Equities do much better, but are prone to high volatility. Is there an asset class that we can substitute for bonds and equities so that we can at least maintain a real increase in inflation-adjusted terms? The long-term inflation hedges have been traditionally gold and property. Gold, however, is something of a faded star. It is not particularly liquid, offers no yield, and is subject to such a variety of non-investment variables that it cannot be relied on to act in a rational way even if inflation does accelerate. Property may be a more reliable inflation hedge, but it is difficult to deal in and requires specialist knowledge. It is also hard to price, and when the market turns down it is almost impossible to sell at any sensible level.

What is required is an investment medium which can be used to produce gains irrespective of whether the market is rising or falling. Hedge funds seem to offer a part solution. In the US, they are already making their way into pension fund portfolios, albeit slowly. If they perform well in the next global bear market, they will undoubtedly be considered more and more as a bona fide asset class by pension fund trustees. As with all things, those who move in first will probably make the best gains; just as managers who backed the emerging markets in the late 1980s are now sitting on large profits.

The argument in favour of hedge funds as a legitimate component of any pension fund portfolio can be summarised as follows:

- Hedge funds offer better risk adjusted returns than conventional bond or equity portfolios.

- The better funds have higher Sharpe Ratios than the major equity markets and, by inference, most fund managers.

- Hedge funds pursue strategies which often produce very low correlations with the major investment stockmarkets and therefore offer exceptionally good diversification of risk characteristics.

Since a well constructed portfolio of hedge funds can be shown to offer better long-term returns with lower volatility than the median pension fund portfolio, the inclusion of hedge funds in an actual scheme will enhance its overall return. This should reduce the scheme's required funding level. It also reduces financial pressure on the parent company, since in the US and the UK the onus has been placed more firmly on the parent company to make good any shortfall in the pension fund's assets. The move to less volatile returns through the use of hedge funds should be welcomed.

The arguments against including hedge funds in these schemes include:

- In many cases the funds are not liquid, and may only deal on a monthly or quarterly basis.

- Redemption notification may have to be given some days ahead of the next dealing date and proceeds may not be received until a month or even more later.

- Force majeure may also come into play if a large number of investors wish to redeem at the same time, and the fund is already committed to a number of illiquid trades from which it cannot extricate itself.

- Hedge funds do occasionally blow up. In the worst cases, all of the assets can be lost.

- Traditional portfolio optimisation techniques are not really suitable for hedge funds because of the total failure concept.

The last two points, as highlighted earlier, matter most. When the Granite Fund collapsed, it was engaged in mortgage-related swaps and was over-geared. As the markets in these securities fell, the fund could not sell. Losses compounded at a frightening rate, and the fund failed and went into liquidation. Investors got nothing back. This was not the only high profile failure in 1994, and shows that when things go wrong they can lead to a total loss. It could happen again, but it is almost inconceivable that a conventional equity or bond fund could fail in the same way.

The final point was also covered in the previous chapter. Total risk considerations must put a limit on the size of holdings of individual hedge funds, making the application of **Modern Portfolio Theory** or even **Post Modern Portfolio Theory** portfolio optimisations partially inappropriate. The percentage of a pension fund's assets held in any hedge fund must be reined back to a level where any collapse could not materially damage the ability of the scheme to meet its liabilities.

In Figure 8.2, on page 192, we show the average performance of various hedge fund strategies relative to major indices over the five years to the end of 1995. The table clearly supports the view that hedge funds are a bona fide investment class for pension funds and should be included in the average portfolio. It is hard to judge the appropriate degree of hedge fund exposure, since there is still insufficient practical experience. Weighting the hedge fund content as heavily as the data suggests might be taking an unexpected risk. We suspect, however, that a weighting of up to 15% spread across 15-20 funds would not be unreasonable.

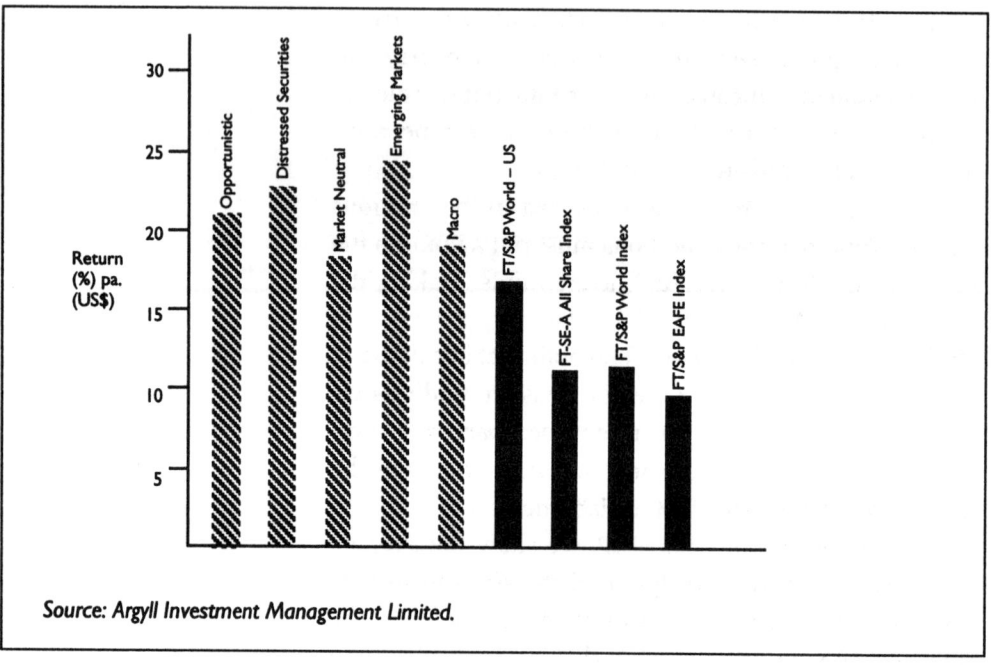

Source: Argyll Investment Management Limited.

Figure 8.2 Hedge Funds Vs Major Indices in US$ over 5 years to end 1995.

Leaving aside pure investment considerations, the real restraint on the growth of this asset class in UK pension funds will be the behaviour of the actuaries. They have a tight grip on pension fund investment mandates, and many may be concerned at the thought of investing in hedge funds. In spite of figures demonstrating that a well diversified hedge fund portfolio would outperform a conventional equity/bond fund in the medium term, the actuaries might still be reluctant to support such a strategy at present. Their attitude is neither surprising nor unreasonable, given the relatively limited data so far available. Those at the leading edge of asset/liability modelling will no doubt begin to include hedge fund strategies in their models once more history is available.

There is a strong case for including hedge fund strategies in mainstream UK pension fund management. If, as we suspect, returns from conventional investments are held back over the next few years, the benefit of such a diversification should enhance performance significantly. By the very nature of their low correlation with traditional assets, the reduction in risk will add another beneficial dimension.

INSURANCE FUNDS

Insurance companies in the UK are heavily regulated in what assets they can buy to cover the liabilities they assume when writing insurance. The Department of Trade and Industry sets rigid guidelines on permissible assets, and on how each asset can be used to match liability. For instance, in the life insurance sector, gilts and other allowable bonds must match the maturity profile of the underwriting book. For property and commercial insurance, the rules are less rigid. Even so, most insurance companies tend to weight their portfolios heavily towards fixed interest. Equities come in, but only in a limited way. The scope does exist for using hedge funds from an investment and actuarial point of view, but the DTI is unlikely to relax and allow such instruments for some time.

The offshore captive insurance market is different. Here the rules governing permitted assets are much looser, and captive companies tend to be more advanced in the way they use equities to give superior long-term investment returns. There is considerable scope to use hedge funds as a substitute for bonds, whilst retaining the equity component. This trend looks sure to grow in the years ahead. The lower risk profile of a well diversified hedge fund portfolio makes an ideal investment for any insurance company seeking consistent low volatility returns.

CONCLUSION

Hedge funds are suitable for most investors if portfolios are constructed with care, and a proper balance between risk and return is maintained. There is no reason why any investor should not hold some hedge funds in his portfolio, unless he requires a high degree of liquidity. On a blind tasting, given only the barest details of performance and risk, most investors would be more than happy to hold these funds. It is only the "hedge fund" label which might put them off.

9

THE
FUTURE

We are about to witness the birth of hedge funds as a new class of investment asset in the UK. They will make a pronounced impact on the investment community, given time. On a risk/return basis, they will challenge the position of conventional unit trusts and investment trusts. They will impact on the pensions industry as schemes become more adept at matching their required returns within an acceptable risk/volatility framework. The insurance industry will be able to look away from fixed interest investment and its dreadful performance record towards more consistent and higher returns, and that should be reflected in lower insurance premiums for customers.

In today's society, once a demand arises, it is very quickly satisfied. The demand for hedge funds will develop as more is written about them, and understanding is advanced. In the US and the UK, there is already considerable data and analysis available, although it is primarily aimed at professional investors. As financial journalists become more aware of the true nature and significance of these funds, they will be able to comment on them far more knowledgeably. A string of newsletters has sprung up in the US, and the UK will eventually follow suit.

It will be commonplace for UK private investors to hold hedge funds in their portfolio in twenty years' time. It has taken a mighty onslaught from the unit trust houses to convince investors to buy their products rather than keep money in the building society. Ultimately those same investors who now hold unit trusts will be persuaded to move part of their investments into hedge funds, attracted by their better risk/return characteristics. These investors will feel more comfortable investing in low/medium risk skill funds exhibiting lower volatility than their roller coaster unit trust equivalents. This could well lead to yet more funds flowing out of traditional safe havens like the building societies.

Pension fund trustees, too, will come to appreciate the benefits of some exposure to hedge funds. If the UK stockmarket's annual real returns trend back to their long-term average of around 3-4%, we are in for some relatively boring times. Bond yields have been in a secular downtrend since inflation peaked in 1975 at 24.9%, and it is not unreasonable to suggest that we have nearly seen the best from this investment category and a reversal must occur in the foreseeable future. When bond yields reverse, prices can only fall. Bonds have been an appalling investment over the years, yet have been held in pension funds because they have been considered safe, low-risk investments. This is absurd. They have little place in any pension fund portfolio. In reality, they are high-risk, low return investments, unlikely to meet any sensible actuarial benchmark over the long term.

If bond returns turn negative or, at best, offer little

real gain, and equities begin to trend back to their normal lower long-term returns, pension scheme funding will have to be stepped up. This will restrain growth in company earnings and share prices, and that will impact on investment returns. It would be unwise to overplay this argument, but it does suggest that institutional investors may begin hunting for more interesting investments if returns from conventional ones begin to wilt.

Insurance companies will also gradually accept these new tools as they are integrated into mainstream investment thinking. Unfortunately the liquidity require-ments and the arcane views of the DTI may heighten resistance to change among insurance companies. The idea of replacing even the most modest proportion of investment in gilts may be construed as adding "risk" no matter what the evidence suggests.

This ignores the case in favour of skill funds. The risk/return profile of various hedge fund strategies compared to stockmarket indices clearly demonstrates the potential value of these funds. There is now ample evidence to suggest that private client and institutional managers in the UK should dip their toes in the water and gain experience of hedge funds. There are also strong arguments in favour of the way they diversify risk, since many hedge funds have low correlations with conventional assets. The problem is that private investors do not yet have the means to get to these funds, while institutional investors are unlikely to consider devoting resources to reviewing the position until market pressures force them to act. In the short term, the pioneering work for both parties must be done by others who have already seen the potential.

Nevertheless, there are moves afoot. Progress is being made. In the US, hedge funds are now an accepted asset. They are held in many portfolios both private and institutional, including those bearing such household names as the Rockefeller Foundation.

There are great changes to come in the hedge fund industry over the next 20 years:

- The most successful funds will grow very large, and eventually their performance will tail off. We have started to witness this already.

- Some funds will reach critical mass, and the laws of diminishing returns will come into play, prompting managers to close their funds to new subscribers.

- Only the macro strategies, dealing in index futures and currencies, will be able to cope with huge cash flow because of the high liquidity of the markets in which these funds invest. Consequently these funds will dominate. In contrast bottom-up micro strategies will be constrained by the narrow markets in which they specialise. The more specialist the player the narrower the market. Some managers may find they are restricted to as little as US$50 million before size proves a drawback.

- The number of funds available will continue to increase significantly, particularly in Europe, as people see the benefits of enhanced all round performance and fund managers see how lucrative the area can be.

- The median hedge fund returns relative to long-only investors will fall as more players enter the field, and average skill levels drop. Leverage will increase to counter this. In turn, this will diminish the risk/return characteristic of this asset class.

- The range of performance will widen in all style groups and a number of funds will continue to be wound up each year as a result of poor performance.

- The increasing number of funds will lead to greater competition. Fees will fall for newcomers without a track record.

- As the percentage of individual and institutional assets held in hedge funds increases the authorities will increase regulation directly or indirectly. This will lead to greater disclosure of portfolio positions.

- Greater regulation will bring increased acceptance that this is a genuine and acceptable asset class for all types of investors.

- Conventional and hedge fund boundaries will merge and a continuum will form.

These changes will not unfold overnight, even at today's accelerated rates of change. The results will be positive for the investment community for a variety of reasons. People will begin to question more thoroughly why they are paying such high fees for "active" long-only management, particularly since a large proportion of such portfolios is effectively indexed anyway. We have gone part of the way already. There are index funds which charge small fees to replicate the return on the index. But they do not improve its risk.

Hedge funds provide the next step – a complementary product which offers returns which are better than the index returns, and which carry lower risk. This is worth paying for. Unless the UK fund management industry realises this and acts, the fleeter of foot will gain an advantage. By promoting an index/hedge fund approach, they will begin to drive down fee levels in conventional pension fund business. When hedge funds can be sold in more user friendly packages to domestic investors, the pressure on traditional unit trust managers will intensify, margins will fall, and the number of funds will contract. Those groups which are slow to pick this up will experience sharp falls in revenue. Unless they cut back or change their investment style, they will be in trouble.

For anyone with an open mind, the sky is the limit. The opportunities are huge and the rewards far superior to those from conventional forms of investment management. Theoretically professional investors will start to allocate cash to high alpha strategies. They will avoid putting capital into markets where there is little opportunity to capture alpha, gaining exposure cheaply by using futures.

In the UK, the greatest benefits will probably go to those who embrace these funds early. Hedge fund returns will fall as more players enter the field and average skill levels drop. The charge will be led by the smaller firms. Larger management groups, entrenched in conventional styles, will not adapt quickly enough – either to offer the products themselves or to retain those still capable of launching funds themselves. The opportunity is available now – seize it.

Make no mistake. Hedge funds are coming.

* * *

GLOSSARY

Absolute returns	returns unrelated and independent of any index measure of performance (see Relative gain).
Absolute benchmark	is a figure which has been set at a specific value and does not vary. It is often set at the commencement of an investment programme as the target rate of return.
Absolute investing	this style of investing aims to achieve consistent positive returns with no losses. It's not influenced by either a market index or competitors' returns. The investor aims to achieve less volatile returns than the stockmarket and so is often likely to do less well in strongly rising bull markets but conversely would not expect to achieve negative results in bear markets.
Alpha	this is the non-systematic risk element of a portfolio. By hedging out systematic market risk we are left with Alpha.
Arbitrage	taking advantage of differentials in the price of a security or currency usually in two different markets to make certain profits.
Bear	an individual who believes that the value of a share, future or option will go down.
Beta	a measure of risk/volatility of a stock relative to the market.
Bull	an individual who believes that the value of a share, future or option will go up.
Correlation	a relationship between two variables, measured on a scale between -1 and 1 where -1 is negative and 1 is positive.
Correlation matrix	a table showing the correlations between a number of individual funds.
Cost of carry premium	an inputed charge related to interest rates.
Distribution	this is a statistical term which explains how a particular variable is spread across a group of people or funds etc. For instance in the case of people we may talk about the distribution of IQs across a class of children and for funds how their returns vary. The shape of the distributions, whether they are normal or skewed, gives us information about the overall nature of the group.

Downside loss   this is the loss which occurs below the Minimum Acceptable Return.

Downside risk   this measures the probability of not achieving a set MAR (see page 203) and also measures the size of the expected average shortfall.

Drawdown   percentage loss during a given period.

Duration   applies to bonds and is a measure of risk/volatility similar to the Beta of an equity.

Efficient frontier   a curve which describes the optimal composition of a portfolio of assets to achieve the lowest level of risk for each possible return.

Futures   these are investments traded on an exchange and allow an investor to buy or sell exposure to a financial index or commodity to create a long or short position in the underlying investment. Futures are dealt in contracts, each of which represents a specific amount of the underlying investment. They are also dealt on margin which means that an investor does not have to pay or produce collateral for the full value of the exposure, long or short, he is taking when he deals. For a relatively small outlay he can gain much larger exposure than the cash deposited as the initial margin. Final settlement occurs on a preset date which can be many months ahead of the transaction although positions can be bought and sold in between. Futures are known as derivatives because they are derived from the underlying primary investment.

Gearing   equivalent to the US term leverage. It is the ratio of money borrowed divided by the capital base used to secure the borrowings. It is usually stated as a percentage eg. 300% in the case where borrowings are 3 times capital.

Hedge fund   an absolute return vehicle managed by entrepreneurial managers which aims to achieve the highest return for a given level of risk.

Limited partnership   a US legal term for a collection of partners in a partnership which consists of 99 partners and 1 managing partner.

Long exposure   the size of the total holding of shares or investments measured by either the number of shares or by the monetary value. Net long exposure is measured after deducting the short positions, if any, from the long exposure.

Long-only manager a manager who only holds long positions in shares/commodities and will never short-sell shares/commodities he does not own.

Long position this occurs when an investor has purchased a holding of shares/commodities which has resulted in him having a net positive exposure to that investment.

Macro-strategies these relate to major issues such as changes in interest rates, expected higher inflation or a change in government.

Micro-strategies these relate to issues specific to an individual company independent of factors which affect the market.

Minimum Acceptable Return (MAR) this is the lowest return which an investor is prepared to accept as a reward for investing in an asset which has risk attached to it. The MAR is often taken as the return on short-dated government bonds.

Modern Portfolio Theory this theory assumes that investors want the least possible dispersion of returns for a given level of gain. Standard deviation (see page 205) is used to measure dispersion.

Non-systematic risk the risk or behaviour which is a characteristic of an individual share and cannot be explained by market risk.

Offshore vehicle an investment company which has been set up in, and is managed from, a low tax rate jurisdiction, eg. the Cayman Islands, Bermuda.

Options the right but not the obligation to buy (a call) or sell (a put) a share at a given price within a certain period.

Post Modern Portfolio Theory this theory assumes that investors want the least downside risk of not achieving their minimum acceptable return (MAR). Semi-variance is the key statistical measure of dispersion of returns.

Prime broker is the service offered by major brokerage houses acting as the focal point for the clearance, settlement, and custody of security trades for a hedge fund.

Qualitative analysis the analysis of a hedge fund/portfolio using the subjective judgement of the manager and the strategy pursued.

Quantitative analysis the analysis of a hedge fund/portfolio using objective statistical techniques.

Relative gain the amount a share or portfolio has increased/fallen in value relative to a set benchmark which is usually a stockmarket index.

Relative investing the investor invests with the intention of achieving a higher return than his benchmark which is often an index, in the case of shares, whose return will vary depending on the time period considered.

Risk-adjusted returns these are returns which reflect the level of risk which was required to achieve them. If two funds have given the same return over a period then the one with the lowest volatility will have the better risk-adjusted return.

Risk profile this is a measure of the level of risk(s) which an investor or group of investors is willing or able to accept. It helps to define the attitude of the investor. Often measured in terms of low, medium and high risk.

Risk/return the relationship between the risk of an investment and its expected gain. Generally the higher the risk the higher its expected gain.

Securities and Exchange Commission (SEC) US regulatory authority.

Semi-variance a statistical measure of how a set of data is spread around its mean. The measure is not necessarily symmetrical about the mean since the distribution may be skewed (see page 205).

Sharpe Ratio the ratio of the return above the MAR divided by the standard deviation. It gives some idea of the return per unit of dispersion risk.

Short position this occurs when an investor has sold shares he does not own. He is said to have "gone short" of the shares thus resulting in a short position.

Short-selling   selling shares not actually owned. The seller sells shares he does not own and hopes that before he has to deliver the stock he will get the chance to buy the shares at a lower price. If the price of the shares does fall he will make an instant profit. If they rise he will have to buy the shares at the higher price and will therefore incur an instant loss.

Skewedness   a statistical measure used to describe the departure of a variable from the normal distribution and which therefore contains biases.

Sortino Ratio   the ratio of the return above the MAR divided by the downside deviation, or the risk of failing to achieve the MAR. It gives an indication of the return per unit of risk in terms of the Post Modern Portfolio Theory.

Standard deviation   a measure of the dispersion of a group of numerical values from the mean. The standard deviation is calculated by taking the differences between each number in the group and the arithmetic average, squaring them to give the variance, summing them and taking the square root.

Stock-picker   an investor who concentrates on buying and selling shares independent of stockmarket trends.

Stop-loss   a way to limit the risk of heavy losses by putting in place a selling order at a pre-set level which is automatically executed if the price of a share falls to that level.

Systematic risk   the dispersion risk inherent in all markets which cannot be diversified.

Upside gain   a gain achieved above the MAR.

Variance   a statistical measure of how a set of data is spread around its mean.

* * *

INDEX

MORE TITLES FROM RUSHMERE WYNNE

The following books published by Rushmere Wynne are part of their finance and investment series.

TRADED OPTIONS - A PRIVATE INVESTOR'S GUIDE: *Peter Temple*
How To Invest More Profitably
Traded Options are investment contracts which give a private investor the opportunity to benefit from changes in share prices at a much lower level of cash commitment. Here they are explained in a step-by-step style. (HB) £16.95

CHARTERS ON CHARTING: An Introduction To Technical Analysis *David Charters*
Charting - or technical analysis as it is often known - is an invaluable guide to making better stockmarket decisions. This guide is illustrated with working examples to enable any private investor to master the subject. (HB) £12.95

PROFIT OF THE PLUNGE: How To Win At Short–Selling *Simon Cawkwell*
Revealing the secrets of the author's success in bear-raiding the Maxwell Corporation, Asil Nadir and many others. He tells how he did it, using the techniques of short-selling and other ways of using the system to make money. (PB) £9.99

PROFIT FROM YOUR PC *David Linton*
A leading PC investment software expert advises on how to buy and set up a PC system and how to use the information to make better stockmarket decisions, including the Internet. (PB) £9.99

THE INDEX OPTION: *Neil Osborne*
The Private Investor's Route to Stockmarket Wealth
A London market trader explains the profitable use of the Index Option for the modern private investor. Book includes free demo disk for Traded Options evaluation program. (HB) £14.99

For further information please write to:
Rushmere Wynne Limited
4 - 5 Harmill, Grovebury Road,
Leighton Buzzard, Beds. LU7 8FF
Tel: 01525 853726 (3 lines)
       01525 850270 (credit card orders)
Fax: 01525 852037